Published in 2009 by Stewart, Tabori & Chang
An imprint of Harry N. Abrams, Inc.

Text copyright © 2009 by Judy Sumner
Photographs copyright © 2009 Yoko Inoue
Illustrations copyright © 2009 Patti Pierce Stone

Library of Congress Cataloging-in-Publication Data:
Sumner, Judy.
Knitted socks east and west : 30 designs inspired by Japanese stitch
patterns / Judy Sumner ; photography by Yoko Inoue.
    p. cm.
ISBN 978-1-58479-799-9
1. Knitting--Patterns. 2. Knitting--Japan. 3. Socks. I. Title.
TT825.S84 2009
746.43'20432--dc22
2008049041

Editor: Melanie Falick
Designer: Onethread
Production Manager: Jacqueline Poirier

The text of this book was composed in Archer.

Printed and bound in China.
10 9 8 7 6 5 4 3 2 1

harry n. abrams, inc.
a subsidiary of La Martinière Groupe

115 West 18th Street
New York, NY 10011
www.hnabooks.com

Knitted Socks East & West

30 Designs Inspired by Japanese Stitch Patterns

Judy Sumner

Photographs by
Yoko Inoue

STC CRAFT/A MELANIE FALICK BOOK
STEWART, TABORI & CHANG
NEW YORK

table of contents

introduction

I have been knitting for sixty years and collecting stitch dictionaries for much of that time, but a couple of years ago, I discovered something new. I found mention of a Japanese stitch dictionary on an online knitting list and, my curiosity piqued, I sought it out. About a month later, *Knitting Patterns Book 250* (Nihon Vogue) arrived in the mail, and a whole new world of knitting opened to me.

I'd seen Japanese knitting magazines and had even taken a class on reading Japanese patterns, but I had never seen stitches like the ones in this book. I had a shelf full of stitch guides, but this one opened my eyes to a whole new realm of possibilities. The stitches were extraordinarily beautiful and exquisitely crafted. Poring over the pages, I couldn't help but wonder where they had come from, and how long they had been around. Whose mind had seen something—a flower, or a butterfly—and been able to translate it into the ornate and complicated pattern in front of me? I marveled that someone had the patience to work out these patterns, as many were not intuitive, requiring a close reading of the stitches as they emerged on the needles.

I remember how excited I was when I opened the book and began looking at the stitch charts. They were quite complex, many with very long stitch repeats and with thirty-two or more different rows—I even saw one that had sixty! Furthermore, while some of the symbols on the charts were familiar to me, many were brand new.

Having deciphered the charts, I jumped to the exciting task of designing with them. A longtime sock designer, I was eager to put these new stitches to use in my favorite medium—I felt I could easily write hundreds of patterns. As the number of socks grew, people kept saying, "You should write a book." I'd been thinking of doing so, but now I knew what would make my sock book different than the many that were already on the shelves—it would introduce Western sock knitters to stitches and techniques they had never seen before.

I consider myself something of an expert in knitting, but the new symbols and techniques I encountered made me feel like an explorer in a new land. And while many of these stitch patterns utilized techniques I recognized from Western knitting, some had their own peculiar take on familiar techniques, and some called for techniques that were new to me. Because of factors such as these, it often took me a very long time to translate a Japanese pattern, and in some socks, I modified design elements to be more like those familiar to Western knitters. I have also adapted the charts in this book to use symbols familiar to Western knitters, and for those who prefer the written word, I've provided the stitch patterns in text format, as well. Japanese knitters might find that I have not performed some stitches the way they do, and it's true that I'm not an expert in their knitting style, having puzzled these techniques out for myself. But the journey has been worth taking nonetheless, and I'm pleased to be able to share the results with you.

In the process of writing this book, what began as a foray into Japanese knitting turned into a crash course in Japanese culture as well. It seemed appropriate to name each sock for some aspect of Japanese culture, so I started by thinking of Japanese words I knew—like *haiku* or *origami*. Then, with the help of resources ranging from a list of Japanese Scrabble words to the Internet, I set out to assign an appropriate name to each sock design. I soon found myself as fascinated with the history and traditions of Japan as I was with the stitch patterns. Researching each word was like following a path: I'd begin by either choosing a stitch pattern that seemed to fit a word I wanted to research—like the wrapped stitch that resembled the *obi* belt worn around a kimono—or by

My first task was to figure out what those Japanese symbols meant. Yes, there were diagrams in the back of the book that illustrated the stitches behind these unusual symbols, but in many cases, they were not immediately clear to me. I spent the next six months staring at those charts and trying to translate them into English words. After that time, my eye doctor informed me that my eyes tested better than they had during the last visit—a hidden benefit to reading charts so closely. I became so enchanted with the Japanese stitch books that each time I was able to find another one, I immediately bought it, adding *Knitting Patterns Book 300* and *Knitting Patterns 500* to my collection.

Most of the stitch patterns used in this book have large repeats, so to add or subtract a repeat would result in a leg circumference that would be either much too large or much too small. Fortunately, these patterns are often quite elastic and will stretch to accommodate a larger circumference. If you are concerned about whether the leg of a particular sock will fit you, consider experimenting with a larger or smaller needle size to increase or decrease the circumference.

Adjusting the circumference of the foot requires a little bit of math, but is fairly simple to do. First, measure your foot at its widest point. Subtract 1" from this measurement, and you have your target circumference. Second, multiply this number by the stitch gauge given in the pattern to determine how many stitches you will need to have on the needles after the gusset decreases are complete.

If the number of stitches left at the end of the gusset section in the pattern is greater than what you need, simply work additional gusset decreases to get to your target number. If the number of stitches is smaller than what you need, work fewer decreases. Finally, once you have completed the foot and are ready to shape the toe, you will need to adjust the number of decreases you work in order to arrive at the final number of stitches given in the pattern. In order to complete the decreases in the length in the pattern (usually 1½" to 2"), you may also need to adjust the number of rows between decreases, working fewer rows if you have more decreases to make, and more rows if you have fewer decreases to make.

searching for a word that seemed to describe a pattern—like the strings on the lutelike *biwa*. One simple word would lead me to the far corners of the Internet, and often through thousands of years of history. I began to see how richly Japanese culture was influenced by spirituality, nature, and beauty. The introductions to each pattern will give you a brief glimpse into some aspect of Japanese culture represented by the accompanying sock design.

As many travelers have discovered, the desire to keep exploring can become addictive. As thrilled as I am to explore the world of Japanese stitches, I can't help but wonder what else is out there, just waiting to be discovered. Do you suppose Chinese knitters, for example, have their own cache of stitch patterns? I've never seen any, but I bet they exist. What fun it would be to discover country after country of new stitch patterns!

I would like to invite you to join me in my travels through these amazing techniques and the Japanese culture, and I hope you find inspiration to push your knitting knowledge by learning new stitches—such as the pkok, the twist/slip, the three-stitch lift, and the wonderfully simple, yet elegant wrap. I have attempted to provide something for everyone—from simple to complex, from short to long, from fine to bulky, and from standard to very unusual. Whether you want elegant lace stockings to wear while lounging or thick socks for your hiking boots, I hope you find what you are looking for.

japanese stitch techniques

As you work through the patterns in this book, you may be surprised to discover how similar many of the techniques are to ones you already know. Twisted stitches, lace stitches, cables, and bobbles are found in Japanese knitting as readily as Western knitting, but often are executed with a particularly Japanese twist.

In addition, you'll find—as I did—a handful of stitches that are brand new, such as the pkok, wraps, three-stitch lift, and a variation on the twisted stitch. In this section, I explain these new stitches and lead you through them step by step.

East Meets West
Many of the techniques used in Japanese stitch patterns are ones Western knitters are familiar with already. For example, many of us have worked the classic feather and fan or old shale patterns, consisting of regular repeats of lacy scallops, constructed with a pattern of increases and decreases. Among the Japanese stitch patterns, I found new variations of this longtime favorite. Two of them are included in the Japanese Fan Tabi (page 57) and Kaiso (page 113) sock patterns.

I also found a lot of twisted stitches used in these patterns—single stitches knitted through the back as well as two stitches twisted together and moving to the right or left. These sorts of stitches are also used in many other places familiar to Western knitters, especially German and Bavarian stitch designs. Somehow, though, the Japanese manage to set them apart by adding a touch of something else—a bit of lace, for example, as in the Biwa socks (page 105).

The Japanese patterns contain a lot of lace, and they often have a floral theme or reflect nature in some way. Some of these patterns can be very complex, but even the simpler ones are quite impressive when worked. For example, the Kimono Lace socks (page 109) mostly consist of a simple pattern of yarnovers and decreases, typical of lace. But a cablelike stitch also appears regularly, adding rhythm and interest. Simpler sock designs—those that consist of basic knit and purl stitches—will often have a few yarnovers and decreases tossed in as well, making the finished effect extraordinary (see Ninja [page 31] and Tatami [page 117]). As in Western knitting, there are cables, but they are often mixed with something I refer to as garter lace—rows of garter stitch separated by rows of yarnovers and decreases that add a decorative touch (see Kyoto Cable [page 97] and Biwa [page 105]).

And finally, there are bobbles. In Japanese patterns, these tricky little bumps pop up in unexpected places. In my Japanese pattern books, many different methods for making bobbles were used. For example, in one version, five stitches were increased from one, then worked for several rows and decreased, resulting in a very "fat" bobble. Another version used a crochet hook to chain five stitches, which were then joined to the original stitch with a slip stitch.

For simplicity's sake, I have written these sock patterns using my own favorite bobble technique: knit in the front, back, front, back, and front of one stitch, then pass four stitches over the stitch on the left. You'll find bobbles in Ikebana (page 35), Karatsu (page 81), and Karaoke (page 125).

Uniquely Japanese

Despite the similarities to Western knitting patterns, however, the Japanese stitch patterns incorporate a few techniques that were brand new to me, and perhaps will be to you, too. Once I deciphered them, I named them pkok (fondly referred to as "peacocks"), wrap, three-stitch lift, and the twist/slip stitch, for the purposes of this book. Illustrated instructions for these techniques appear on pages 12-15.

Pkok

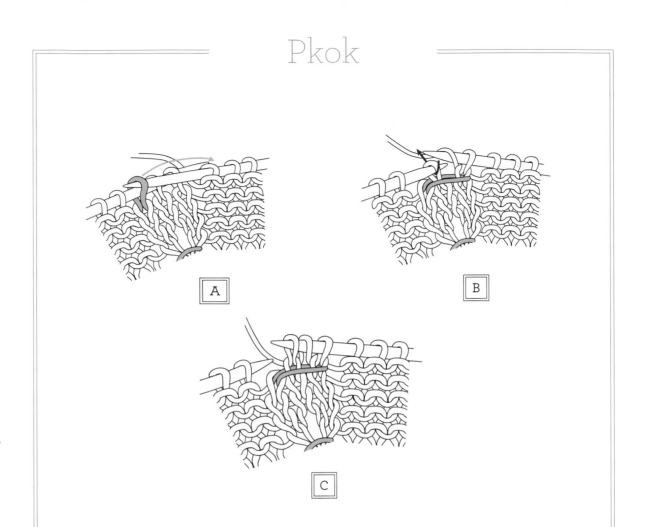

When I saw this stitch in the Japanese stitch dictionaries, I thought it looked like a lacy chain. I found several variations in my Japanese books, but for all of the socks shown in this book, I used this basic one, which is made over three stitches:

Step 1: Using your right-hand needle, pick up the third stitch on the left-hand needle, pass it over the first two stitches, and let it drop off the needle (A).

Step 2: Knit a stitch, yarnover, knit a stitch. This is done every fourth row/round, and the three stitches are worked in Stockinette stitch on intervening rows/rounds (B and C).

Designs using this technique are Ikebana (page 35), Fuji Pedicure (page 45), Shiatsu (page 49), Bonsai (page 61), Hanami Lace (page 85), Obi Yoga (page 89), and Karaoke (page 125).

Wrap

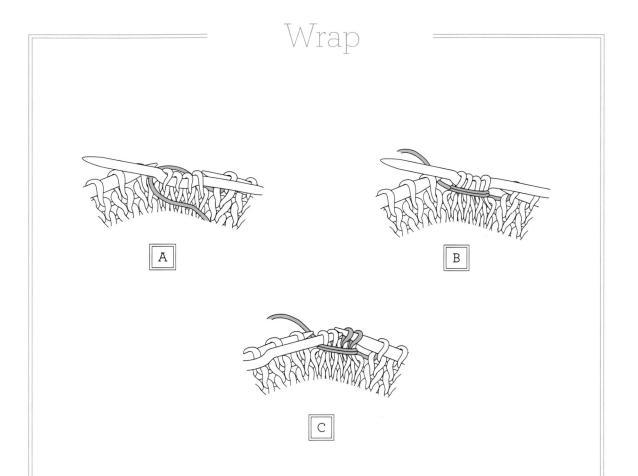

I have seen wrapped stitches used in knitting patterns in the past, but never to this degree. Stitches may be wrapped as few as two times and as many as five. And each time, you might wrap anywhere from three stitches to fourteen!

Step 1: Place the stitches to be wrapped (your pattern will tell you how many) on a short cable or double-pointed needle (A).

Step 2: Wrap your yarn around these stitches in a counterclockwise direction, using the number of wraps called for in the pattern (B).

Step 3: Knit the stitches (or work as indicated in pattern) off the cable or double-pointed needle, and continue the pattern (C).

Designs using this method include Shiatsu (page 49), Karatsu (page 81), and Inro Hiking (page 93).

Twist/Slip Stitch

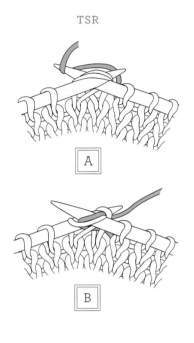

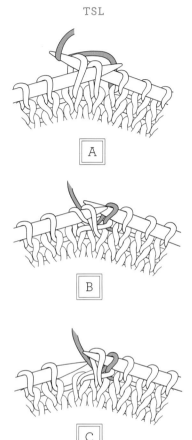

The twist/slip maneuver (TSL and TSR) is very similar to the familiar method of twisting two stitches together and knitting them so the front stitch leans to the right or left, usually abbreviated as LT or RT. However, in this case, only one of the stitches is actually knitted; the other is slipped. The result, much like the LT or RT, is a stitch that moves to the right or the left.

The TSR (above left) is worked by beginning as you would with RT. Insert the right-hand needle into two stitches on the left-hand needle as if to knit them together (A). Then pull the yarn only through the first stitch (B) and allow the second stitch to just slip

to the right-hand needle without knitting it (C). The slipped stitch is knit on the second round, creating an elongated stitch that clearly leans to the right.

The TSL (above right) is worked by beginning as you would with the LT. However, you insert the right-hand needle into the back of the second stitch and pull the yarn through to knit it (A and B), then insert your needle into the front stitch as if to purl and slip it (C). This slipped stitch is knit on the following round, and the resulting stitch leans to the left.

Konnichiwa (page 19) uses these techniques.

Three-Stitch Lift

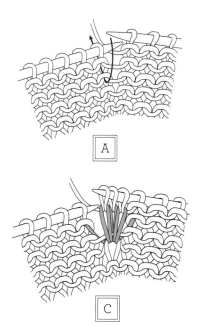

A

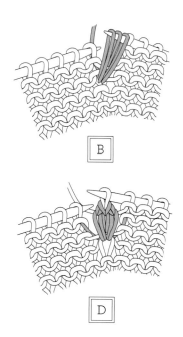

B

C

D

This was the trickiest technique of all to figure out. After months of experimentation, I finally discovered that you pick up a stitch, do a yarnover, pick up another stitch, and then drop the stitch on your left-hand needle. The final part of the technique turned out to be something pretty simple—a centered double decrease, often referred to as s2kp2 (slip two stitches as if to knit two together, knit one, and pass the two slipped stitches over the knit stitch, which leaves the center stitch on the top).

Step 1 (Round 1): With yarn in back, using your right-hand needle, go through the stitch three rows below the next stitch on the left-hand needle, pick up the yarn, and pull it through the stitch (A).

Step 2: Yarnover.

Step 3: Go through the same stitch as you did in Step 1, pick up the yarn, and pull it through the stitch. You now have three working stitches on your right-hand needle (B).

Drop the next stitch on your left-hand needle (it's anchored three rows down so it won't get away from you).

Note: Technically, the Three-Stitch Lift is completed after Step 3; however, Steps 4 and 5 (included in the pattern text and charts in the two rounds following the Three-Stitch Lift round) tell you how to work the two extra stitches that were created in Steps 1-3.

Step 4 (Round 2): When you reach the three lifted stitches on the next round, either knit or purl them, depending on your pattern instructions (C). (You will have two extra stitches for each lift worked on this round.)

Step 5 (Round 3): When you reach these three stitches on the following round, work s2kp2, the centered double decrease, across these stitches. You will now be back to your original number of stitches (D).

Designs using the three-stitch lift are Japanese Garden (page 41), Haiku (page 53), and Geisha Lounge (page 65).

projects

16

konnichiwa

Konnichiwa is the Japanese greeting that means "good day," and I greet you as you enter the first pattern in my book. In Japanese culture, greetings are very important, and at a young age Japanese children are taught to offer them with enthusiasm. In that spirit, I offer these Konnichiwa socks to you.

I chose these socks to introduce you to a Japanese stitch that was new to me, and which I refer to as a "twist/slip." You are probably familiar with two stitches twisted to the right or left. This is a similar maneuver, but instead of knitting both of the stitches, one is knitted and one is slipped, creating an elongated stitch that provides a defined line. Once you master this technique, these comfortable socks are very easy and quick to knit.

FINISHED MEASUREMENTS
8½" Foot circumference
10½" Foot length from back of Heel
9¾" Leg length to base of Heel

YARN
Blue Sky Alpacas Worsted Hand Dyes
(50% alpaca / 50% merino wool; 100 grams /
100 yards): 3 hanks #2100 Blue Jeans

NEEDLES
One set of five double-pointed needles
(dpn) size US 6 (4 mm)
Change needle size if necessary to obtain
correct gauge.

NOTIONS
Stitch marker

GAUGE
17 sts and 25 rnds = 4" (10 cm) in
Stockinette stitch (St st)

ABBREVIATIONS
TSL (twist/slip left): Knit into back loop of second st, then insert tip of right-hand needle into front of first st as if to purl, slip both sts from needle together, allowing first st to be slipped rather than knit (see page 14).
TSR (twist/slip right): Insert right-hand needle into next 2 sts as if to k2tog, draw up a loop, bring tip of right-hand needle out through first st only, slip both sts from needle together, allowing second st to be slipped rather than knit (see page 14).

STITCH PATTERNS

PATTERN A
(multiple of 10 sts; 2-rnd repeat)
Rnd 1: *[P2, k2] twice, p2; repeat from * to end.
Rnd 2: *K4, p2, k4; repeat from * to end.
Repeat Rnds 1 and 2 for Pattern A.

PATTERN B
(multiple of 10 sts; 14-rnd repeat)
Rnds 1 and 3: Knit.
Rnds 2 and 4: *P2, k6, p2; repeat from * to end.
Rnd 5: *K2, TSL, k2, TSR, k2; repeat from * to end.
Rnds 6 and 12: *P3, k4, p3; repeat from * to end.
Rnd 7: *K3, TSL, TSR, k3; repeat from * to end.
Rnds 8 and 10: *P4, k2, p4; repeat from * to end.
Rnd 9: *K4, TSL, k4; repeat from * to end.
Rnd 11: *K3, TSR, TSL, k3; repeat from * to end.
Rnd 13: *K2, TSR, k2, TSL, k2; repeat from * to end.
Rnd 14: Repeat Rnd 2.
Repeat Rnds 1-14 for Pattern B.

LEG
CO 40 sts. Divide sts evenly among 4 needles (10-10-10-10). Join for working in the rnd, being careful not to twist sts; place marker (pm) for beginning of rnd. Begin Pattern A; work even for 10 rnds.
Next Rnd: Change to Pattern B; work even until 3 vertical repeats of Pattern B have been completed.

HEEL FLAP
Set-Up Row 1 (RS): K10, turn.
Set-Up Row 2: Slip 1, p19, working all 20 sts onto 1 needle for Heel Flap, and removing marker. Leave remaining 20 sts on 2 needles for instep.
Row 1: Working only on 20 Heel Flap sts, *slip 1, k1; repeat from * to end.
Row 2: Slip 1, purl to end.
Repeat Rows 1 and 2 nine times.

TURN HEEL
Set-Up Row 1 (RS): Slip 1, k11, skp, k1, turn.
Set-Up Row 2: Slip 1, p5, p2tog, p1, turn.
Row 1: Slip 1, knit to 1 st before gap, skp (the 2 sts on either side of gap), k1, turn.
Row 2: Slip 1, purl to 1 st before gap, p2tog (the 2 sts on either side of gap), p1, turn.
Repeat Rows 1 and 2 twice, omitting final k1 and p1 sts in last repeat of Rows 1 and 2–12 sts remain.

GUSSET

Next Row (RS): *Needle 1:* Knit across Heel Flap sts, pick up and knit 11 sts along left side of Heel Flap, M1; *Needles 2 and 3:* Work even in Pattern B as established; *Needle 4:* M1, pick up and knit 11 sts along right side of Heel Flap, k6 from Needle 1. Join for working in the rnd; pm for beginning of rnd–56 sts (18-10-10-18).

Next Rnd: *Needle 1:* Knit to last 2 sts, skp; *Needles 2 and 3:* Work even as established; *Needle 4:* K2tog, knit to end–54 sts remain.

Decrease Rnd: *Needle 1:* Knit to last 3 sts, skp, k1; *Needles 2 and 3:* Work even as established; *Needle 4:* K1, k2tog, knit to end–52 sts remain (16-10-10-16). Work even for 1 rnd. Repeat Decrease Rnd every other rnd 6 times–40 sts remain (10-10-10-10).

FOOT

Work even until Foot measures 9", or 1½" less than desired length from back of Heel.

Next Rnd: Change to St st (knit every rnd) across all sts.

TOE

Decrease Rnd: *Needle 1:* Knit to last 3 sts, skp, k1; *Needle 2:* K1, k2tog, knit to end; *Needle 3:* Knit to last 3 sts, skp, k1; *Needle 4:* K1, k2tog, knit to end–36 sts remain. Knit 1 rnd.

Repeat Decrease Rnd every other rnd 5 times–16 sts remain (4-4-4-4). Knit to end of Needle 1.

FINISHING

Break yarn, leaving long tail. Transfer sts from Needle 1 to Needle 4, and sts from Needle 3 to Needle 2. Using Kitchener st (see General Techniques, page 140), graft Toe sts. Weave in ends. Block lightly.

KEY

☐ Knit

⊡ Purl

⧖ **TSL (twist/slip left):** Knit into back loop of second st, then insert tip of right-hand needle into front of first st as if to purl, slip both sts from needle together, allowing first st to be slipped rather than knit (see page 14).

⧗ **TSR (twist/slip right):** Insert right-hand needle into next 2 sts as if to k2tog, draw up a loop, bring tip of right-hand needle out through first st only, slip both sts from needle together, allowing second st to be slipped rather than knit (see page 14).

PATTERN B

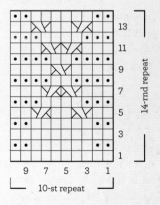

14-rnd repeat

10-st repeat

chouwa

The first reference I found to the word *chouwa* said it could be translated into English as "harmony." I have always felt that the pattern in these socks—an amazing meld of the lacy ripples of feather and fan stitch combined with cables—is symbolic of harmony. Imagine my surprise when I later discovered that this word is the title of a Japanese song that, when translated, includes these lyrics: "In the midst of silence, a single drop causes a ripple that spreads through the water at the bottom of the well."

These Chouwa—or harmony—socks have a simple rolled edge, followed by a short portion of twisted rib stitches that merges into the pleasingly textured pattern of simple cables, decreases, and yarnovers.

FINISHED MEASUREMENTS
8½" Foot circumference
9¼" Foot length from back of Heel
9½" Leg length to base of Heel

YARN
Lisa Souza Hardtwist Merino Petite Yarn (100% hand-dyed merino superwash wool; 100 grams / 500 yards):
1 hank Mulberry

NEEDLES
One set of five double-pointed needles (dpn) size US 1 (2.25 mm)
Change needle size if necessary to obtain correct gauge.

NOTIONS
Stitch marker; cable needle (cn)

GAUGE
30 sts and 44 rnds = 4" (10 cm) in Stockinette stitch (St st)

ABBREVIATIONS
C4F: Slip 2 sts to cn, hold to front, k2, k2 from cn.

KEY

☐ **Knit**

◻ **Yo**

◩ **K2tog**

⬓ **C4F:** Slip 2 sts to cn, hold to front, k2, k2 from cn.

PATTERN B

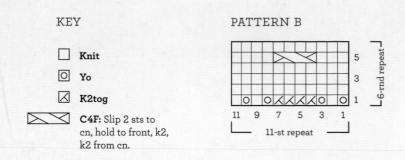

STITCH PATTERNS

PATTERN A
(multiple of 2 sts; 1-rnd repeat)
All Rnds: *K1-tbl, p1; repeat from * to end.

PATTERN B
(multiple of 11 sts; 6-rnd repeat)
Rnd 1: *Yo, k1, yo, [k2tog] 4 times, [yo, k1] twice; repeat from * to end.
Rnds 2-4: Knit.
Rnd 5: *K3, C4F, k4; repeat from * to end.
Rnd 6: Knit.
Repeat Rnds 1-6 for Pattern B.

LEG
CO 66 sts. Divide sts evenly among 3 needles (22-22-22). Join for working in the rnd, being careful not to twist sts; place marker (pm) for beginning of rnd. Begin St st (knit every rnd); work even for 6 rnds.
Next Rnd: Change to Pattern A; work even for 10 rnds.
Next Rnd: Change to Pattern B; work even until piece measures approximately 8" from the beginning, ending with Rnd 6 of pattern

B, and decreasing 2 sts on last rnd–64 sts remain. Redistribute sts among 4 needles (16-16-16-16).

HEEL FLAP
Set-Up Row 1 (RS): K16, turn.
Set-Up Row 2: Slip 1, p31, working all 32 sts onto 1 needle for Heel Flap, and removing marker. Leave remaining 32 sts on 2 needles for instep.
Row 1: *Slip 1, k1; repeat from * to end.
Row 2: Slip 1, purl to end.
Repeat Rows 1 and 2 eleven times.

TURN HEEL
Set-Up Row 1 (RS): Slip 1, k17, skp, k1, turn.
Set-Up Row 2: Slip 1, p5, p2tog, p1, turn.
Row 1: Slip 1, knit to 1 st before gap, skp (the 2 sts on either side of gap), k1, turn.
Row 2: Slip 1, purl to 1 st before gap, p2tog (the 2 sts on either side of gap), p1, turn.
Repeat Rows 1 and 2 five times, omitting final k1 and p1 sts in last repeat of Rows 1 and 2–18 sts remain.

GUSSET
Next Row (RS): *Needle 1:* Knit across Heel Flap sts, pick up and knit 13 sts along left side of Heel Flap, M1; *Needles 2 and 3:* Knit across sts on instep needles; *Needle 4:* M1, pick up and knit 13 sts along right side of Heel Flap, k9 from Needle 1. Join for working in the rnd; pm for beginning of rnd–78 sts (23-16-16-23).
Next Rnd: *Needle 1:* Knit to last 2 sts, skp; *Needles 2 and 3:* Knit; *Needle 4:* K2tog, knit to end–76 sts remain.
Decrease Rnd: *Needle 1:* Knit to last 3 sts, skp, k1; *Needles 2 and 3:* Knit; *Needle 4:* K1, k2tog, knit to end–74 sts remain (21-16-16-21). Work even for 1 rnd.
Repeat Decrease Rnd every other rnd 5 times–64 sts remain (16-16-16-16).

FOOT
Work even until piece measures 7¾", or 1½" less than desired length from back of Heel.

TOE
Decrease Rnd: *Needle 1:* Knit to last 3 sts, skp, k1; *Needle 2:* K1, k2tog, knit to end; *Needle 3:* Knit to last 3 sts, skp, k1; *Needle 4:* K1, k2tog, knit to end–60 sts remain (5-5-5-5). Knit 1 rnd.
Repeat Decrease Rnd every other rnd 10 times–20 sts remain (5-5-5-5). Knit to end of Needle 1.

FINISHING
Break yarn, leaving long tail. Transfer sts from Needle 1 to Needle 4, and sts from Needle 3 to Needle 2. Using Kitchener st (see General Techniques, page 140), graft Toe sts. Weave in ends. Block lightly.

origami

Origami is the Japanese art of paper folding, which spread to Japan from China sometime during the sixth century. Originally, because very little paper was available, only the rich could afford to do paper folding, and their intricately folded objects were used as gifts. As paper became easier to get, origami became a popular art.

The Origami sock looks unusual when it is not on the foot. Worked from the toe up, the leg of the sock appears to have "folds" where it goes in and out, much like the ornate folds of origami. However, when worn, the leg flattens out into a very decorative fabric. Because it is worked with a seventeen-stitch repeat, you have to move two stitches from one needle to another in order to work Round 3, and then move them back at the end to continue the pattern. Other than this maneuver, it is a fairly straightforward lace pattern that uses many yarnovers, twisted stitches, and both right- and left-leaning decreases.

FINISHED MEASUREMENTS
8½" Foot circumference
10½" Foot length from back of Heel
9" Leg length to base of Heel

YARN
ShibuiKnits Sock (100% superwash merino wool; 50 grams / 191 yards): 2 hanks #S1675 Pagoda. *Note: If you work the Foot longer than 10½" from back of Heel, you will need to purchase an additional hank.*

NEEDLES
One set of five double-pointed needles (dpn) size US 1 (2.25 mm)
Change needle size if necessary to obtain correct gauge.

NOTIONS
Stitch marker

GAUGE
30 sts and 46 rnds = 4" (10 cm) in Stockinette stitch (St st)

STITCH PATTERNS

PATTERN A
(multiple of 2 sts; 4-rnd repeat)

Rnd 1: Knit.
Rnd 2: Purl.
Rnd 3: *K2tog, yo; repeat from * to end.
Rnd 4: Purl.
Repeat Rnds 1-4 for Pattern A.

PATTERN B
(multiple of 17 sts; 16-rnd repeat)

Rnd 1: *[K1, yo] 3 times, [ssk] 3 times, [k2tog] 3 times, [yo, k1] twice, yo; repeat from * to end.

Rnds 2 and 4: *[K1-tbl, p1] twice, k2, p6, k2, p1, k1-tbl, p1; repeat from * to end.

Rnd 3: *[K1-tbl, p1] twice, yo, ssk, k6, k2tog, yo, p1, k1-tbl, p1; repeat from * to end.

Rnd 5: *[K1-tbl, p1] twice, k1-tbl, yo, ssk, k4, k2tog, yo, [k1-tbl, p1] twice; repeat from * to end.

Rnd 6: *[K1-tbl, p1] 3 times, k1, p4, k1, [p1, k1-tbl] twice, p1; repeat from * to end.

Rnd 7: *[K1-tbl, p1] 3 times, yo, ssk, k2, k2tog, yo, [p1, k1-tbl] twice, p1; repeat from * to end.

Rnd 8: *[K1-tbl, p1] 3 times, k2, p2, k2, [p1, k1-tbl] twice, p1; repeat from * to end.

Rnd 9: *[K1-tbl, p1] 3 times, k1-tbl, yo, ssk, k2tog, yo, [k1-tbl, p1] 3 times; repeat from * to end.

Rnd 10: *[K1-tbl, p1] 3 times, k1-tbl, k4, [k1-tbl, p1] 3 times; repeat from * to end.

Rnds 11, 13, and 15: *[K1, yo] 3 times, [k2tog] 3 times, [ssk] 3 times, [yo, k1] twice, yo; repeat from * to end.

Rnds 12, 14, and 16: Knit.
Repeat Rnds 1-16 for Pattern B.

TOE

Note: Sock is worked from the toe up.
Holding 2 needles parallel, and using Long-Tail CO (see General Techniques, page 141), *CO 1 st on back needle, then 1 st on front needle; repeat from * 9 times, turn—20 sts (10-10).

Next Rnd: Using third needle, *k1-tbl; repeat from * across front needle, then across back needle, joining to work in the rnd; place marker (pm) for beginning of rnd.

Increase Rnd 1: *Needle 1:* K1, M1-r, knit to last st, M1-l, k1; *Needle 2:* Work as for Needle 1—24 sts. Work even for 1 rnd. Redistribute sts among 4 needles (6-6-6-6).

Increase Rnd 2: *Needle 4:* K1, M1-r, knit to end, reposition marker for beginning of rnd; *Needle 1:* Knit to last st, M1-l, k1; *Needle 2:* K1, M1-r, knit to end; *Needle 3:* Knit to last st, M1-l, k1; knit to end of Needle 4—28 sts.
Repeat Increase Rnd 2 every other rnd 9 times—64 sts (16-16-16-16).

FOOT

Work even until Foot measures 8½", or 2" less than desired length from Toe. Transfer sts from Needle 1 to Needle 4 for Heel, removing marker. Leave remaining 32 sts on 2 needles for instep.

HEEL

Note: Heel is shaped using Short Rows (see General Techniques, page 141).
Short Rows 1 and 2: Working only on 32 Heel sts, knit to last st, wrp-t; purl to last st, wrp-t.

Short Rows 3 and 4: Knit to 1 st before wrapped st from row below previous row, wrp-t; purl to 1 st before wrapped st from row below previous row, wrp-t.
Repeat Short Rows 3 and 4 until 14 sts remain unworked in the center of the Heel.

Short Rows 5 and 6: Knit to first wrapped st from row below previous row, work wrap together with wrapped st, turn; purl to first wrapped st from row below previous row, work wrap together with wrapped st, turn.
Repeat Short Rows 5 and 6 until all Heel sts have been worked.
Next Row (RS): K16, pm for new beginning of rnd.

LEG

Next Rnd: *Needle 1:* K16, M1; *Needles 2 and 3:* Knit, increase 1 st on each needle; *Needle 4:* M1, K16—68 sts.
***Next Rnd:** Redistribute sts (16-18-16-18). Work in Pattern A across all sts; work even for 4 rnds. Knit 2 rnds.
Next Rnd: Redistribute sts (17-17-17-17). Change to Pattern B; work even for 16 rnds.
Repeat from * twice. Knit 1 rnd, decrease 1 st on each needle—64 sts remain.
Next Rnd: Work in Pattern A across all sts, beginning with Rnd 2; work even for 3 rnds.
Next Rnd: Change to Garter st (knit 1 rnd, purl 1 rnd); work even for 6 rnds. BO all sts loosely. Weave in ends. Block lightly.

KEY

- ☐ Knit
- ⊡ Purl
- Ⅱ K1-tbl
- ⊙ Yo
- ⟋ K2tog
- ⟍ Ssk

PATTERN B

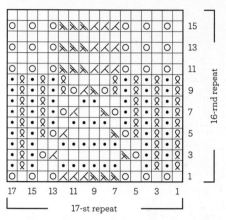

16-rnd repeat
15 13 11 9 7 5 3 1
17 15 13 11 9 7 5 3 1
17-st repeat

ninja

In Japanese history, a ninja was someone specially trained in stealth tactics and a variety of unorthodox arts of war, including assassination, espionage, and various martial arts. Shrouded in mystery and concealment, ninja often camouflaged themselves in dark colors to blend in with the cover of night.

I named these socks Ninja for their complex combination of seed stitches and decreases, their dark color, and the element of surprise created by a bit of lace. At first glance, there is no openwork to be seen; the lace pattern reveals itself when the sock is worn. Although they appear complicated to knit, the Ninja socks use a repeat of relatively basic stitches.

FINISHED MEASUREMENTS
8½" Foot circumference
10" Foot length from back of Heel
7¼" Leg length to base of Heel

YARN
Knit Picks Risata (42% cotton / 39% superwash wool / 13% polyamide / 6% elite elastic; 50 grams / 196 yards): 2 balls #24107 Ash

NEEDLES
One set of five double-pointed needles (dpn) size US 1 (2.25 mm)
Change needle size if necessary to obtain correct gauge.

NOTIONS
Stitch marker

GAUGE
30 sts and 42 rnds = 4"(10 cm) in Stockinette stitch (St st)

KEY

- ☐ Knit
- ⊡ Purl
- ⊡ Yo
- ☒ K2tog
- ☒ Ssk

PATTERN A

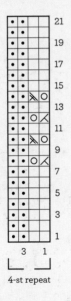

4-st repeat

PATTERN B

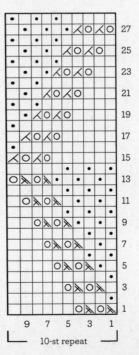

10-st repeat

STITCH PATTERNS

PATTERN A
(multiple of 4 sts)
Rnds 1-7, 9, 11, and 13: *K2, p2;
repeat from * to end.
Rnds 8 and 12: *K2tog, yo, p2;
repeat from * to end.
Rnds 10 and 14: *Yo, ssk, p2;
repeat from * to end.
Rnds 15-21: Repeat Rnd 1.

PATTERN B
(multiple of 10 sts)
Rnd 1: *[Ssk, yo] twice, k6; repeat
from * to end.
Rnds 2 and 4: *P1, k9; repeat from
* to end.
Rnd 3: *K1, [ssk, yo] twice, k5;
repeat from * to end.
Rnd 5: *K1, p1, [ssk, yo] twice, k4;
repeat from * to end.
Rnds 6 and 8: *P1, k1, p1, k7; repeat
from * to end.
Rnd 7: *K1, p1, k1, [ssk, yo] twice,
k3; repeat from * to end.
Rnd 9: *[K1, p1] twice, [ssk, yo]
twice, k2; repeat from * to end.
Rnds 10, 12, and 14: *[P1, k1] twice,
p1, k5; repeat from * to end.
Rnd 11: *[K1, p1] twice, k1, [ssk, yo]
twice, k1; repeat from * to end.
Rnd 13: *[K1, p1] 3 times, [ssk, yo]
twice; repeat from * to end.
Rnd 15: *K6, [yo, k2tog] twice;
repeat from * to end.
Rnds 16 and 18: *K9, p1; repeat
from * to end.
Rnd 17: *K5, [yo, k2tog] twice, k1;
repeat from * to end.
Rnd 19: *K4, [yo, k2tog] twice, p1,
k1; repeat from * to end.
Rnds 20 and 22: *K7, p1, k1, p1;
repeat from * to end.
Rnd 21: *K3, [yo, k2tog] twice, k1,
p1, k1; repeat from * to end.
Rnd 23: *K2, [yo, k2tog] twice,
[p1, k1] twice; repeat from * to end.
Rnds 24 and 26: *K5, [p1, k1]
twice, p1; repeat from * to end.

Rnd 25: *K1, [yo, k2tog] twice, [k1, p1] twice, k1; repeat from * to end.
Rnd 27: *[Yo, k2tog] twice, [p1, k1] 3 times; repeat from * to end.
Rnd 28: Repeat Rnd 24.

LEG

CO 60 sts. Divide sts evenly among 3 needles (20-20-20). Join for working in the rnd, being careful not to twist sts; place marker (pm) for beginning of rnd. Begin Pattern A; work even for 21 rnds.
Next Rnd: Change to Pattern B; work Rnds 1-28 once, then Rnds 1-14 once. Rearrange sts among 4 needles (15-15-15-15).

HEEL FLAP

Set-Up Row 1 (RS): K15, turn.
Set-Up Row 2: Slip 1, p29, working all 30 sts onto 1 needle for Heel Flap, and removing marker. Leave remaining 30 sts on 2 needles for instep.
Row 1: Working only on 30 Heel Flap sts, *slip 1, k1; repeat from * to end.
Row 2: Slip 1, purl to end.
Repeat Rows 1 and 2 eleven times.

TURN HEEL

Set-Up Row 1 (RS): Slip 1, k16, skp, k1, turn.
Set-Up Row 2: Slip 1, p5, p2tog, p1, turn.
Row 1: Slip 1, knit to 1 st before gap, skp (the 2 sts on either side of gap), k1, turn.
Row 2: Slip 1, purl to 1 st before gap, p2tog (the 2 sts on either side of gap), p1, turn.
Repeat Rows 1 and 2 four times–18 sts remain.

GUSSET

Next Row (RS): *Needle 1:* Knit across Heel Flap sts, pick up and knit 13 sts along left side of Heel Flap, M1; *Needles 2 and 3:* Knit across sts on instep needles; *Needle 4:* M1, pick up and knit 13 sts along right side of Heel Flap, k9 from Needle 1. Join for working in the rnd; pm for beginning of rnd–76 sts (23-15-15-23).
Next Rnd: *Needle 1:* Knit to last 2 sts, skp; *Needles 2 and 3:* Knit; *Needle 4:* K2tog, knit to end–74 sts remain.
Decrease Rnd: *Needle 1:* Knit to last 3 sts, skp, k1; *Needles 2 and 3:* Knit; *Needle 4:* K1, k2tog, knit to end–72 sts remain (22-15-15-22). Work even for 1 rnd.
Repeat Decrease Rnd every other rnd 6 times–60 sts remain (15-15-15-15).

FOOT

Work even until Foot measures 8½", or 1½" less than desired length from back of Heel.

TOE

Decrease Rnd: *Needle 1:* Knit to last 3 sts, skp, k1; *Needle 2:* K1, k2tog, knit to end; *Needle 3:* Knit to last 3 sts, skp, k1; *Needle 4:* K1, k2tog, knit to end–56 sts remain. Knit 2 rnds.
Repeat Decrease Rnd every 3 rnds twice, every other rnd 3 times, then every rnd 4 times–20 sts remain (5-5-5-5). Knit to end of Needle 1.

FINISHING

Break yarn, leaving long tail. Transfer sts from Needle 1 to Needle 4, and sts from Needle 3 to Needle 2. Using Kitchener st (see General Techniques, page 140), graft Toe sts. Weave in ends. Block lightly.

ikebana

Ikebana (literally translated as "flowers kept alive") is an ancient form of Japanese flower arranging. Much more than simply arranging flowers in a vase, *ikebana* is considered a "living" art that reflects the Japanese love of nature and brings nature and humans together. It is also considered to have spiritual aspects. As you place the flowers, leaves, branches, and berries in the arrangement, for example, you become quiet and more able to "live in the moment" (fittingly, also a benefit of knitting). There are two basic styles of *ikebana*: one that uses a shallow, flat container and one that uses a tall vase.

I thought this stitch pattern represented a floral arrangement, and I originally envisioned it as the shallow-vase version, with the "flowers" standing in a base (the plain foot). Modified into a kneesock, it now reflects the tall-vase style of *ikebana*, with the arrangement flowing up from the foot. This is one of the more complex designs in this book, with two separate stitch patterns being worked simultaneously. One is a four-stitch pattern that includes the pkok and runs the entire length of the sock. The primary pattern—limited to the leg of the sock, where it is more visible—is much more complex and includes twisted stitches, lace, and bobbles for a look that mimics ferns, vines, and buds or tiny blossoms.

FINISHED MEASUREMENTS
7½" Foot circumference
9½" Foot length from back of Heel
14½" Leg length to base of Heel

YARN
Crystal Palace Yarns Panda Silk
(52% bamboo / 43% superwash merino wool / 5% combed silk; 50 grams / 204 yards): 3 balls #3005 Bamboo Green

NEEDLES
One set of five double-pointed needles (dpn) size US 1 (2.25 mm)
Change needle size if necessary to obtain correct gauge.

NOTIONS
Stitch markers

GAUGE
32 sts and 42 rnds = 4" (10 cm) in Stockinette stitch (St st)

ABBREVIATIONS
MB (Make Bobble): Knit into front, back, front, back, then front of next st to increase to 5 sts; pass second, third, fourth, then fifth st over first st and off needle.
Pkok: Slip third st on left-hand needle over first 2 sts and off needle; k1, yo, k1 (see page 12).

KEY

☐ **Knit**

⊡ **Purl**

⟊ **K1-tbl**

⊙ **Yo**

⟋ **K2tog**

⟍ **Ssk**

⟋ **K3tog**

⬤ **MB:** Knit into front, back, front,
back, then front of next st to
increase to 5 sts; pass second,
third, fourth, then fifth st,
1 at a time, over first st and
off needle.

PATTERN B

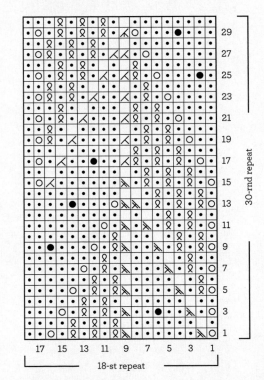

STITCH PATTERNS

PATTERN A
(multiple of 2 sts; 1-rnd repeat)
All Rnds: *K1-tbl, p1; repeat from * to end.

PATTERN B
(multiple of 18 sts; 30-rnd repeat)
Rnd 1: *Yo, ssk, p6, ssk, [k1-tbl, p1] 3 times, yo, p2; repeat from * to end.
Rnd 2: *P1, k1, p6, k1, [k1-tbl, p1] twice, k1-tbl, p4; repeat from * to end.
Rnd 3: *Yo, p1, ssk, p2, MB, p2, ssk, p1, [k1-tbl, p1] twice, yo, p3; repeat from * to end.
Rnd 4: *P2, k1, p5, k1, [p1, k1-tbl] twice, p5; repeat from * to end.
Rnd 5: *Yo, k1-tbl, p1, ssk, p4, ssk, [k1-tbl, p1] twice, yo, p4; repeat from * to end.
Rnd 6: *P1, k1-tbl, p1, k1, p4, k1, k1-tbl, p1, k1-tbl, p6; repeat from * to end.
Rnd 7: *Yo, p1, k1-tbl, p1, ssk, p3, ssk, p1, k1-tbl, p1, yo, p5; repeat from * to end.
Rnd 8: *P2, k1-tbl, p1, k1, p3, k1, p1, k1-tbl, p7; repeat from * to end.
Rnd 9: *Yo, [k1-tbl, p1] twice, ssk, p2, ssk, k1-tbl, p1, yo, p3, MB, p2; repeat from * to end.
Rnd 10: *[P1, k1-tbl] twice, p1, k1, p2, k1, k1-tbl, p8; repeat from * to end.
Rnd 11: *Yo, [p1, k1-tbl] twice, p1, [ssk, p1] twice, yo, p7; repeat from * to end.
Rnd 12: *P2, [k1-tbl, p1] twice, k1, p1, k1, p9; repeat from * to end.

Rnd 13: *Yo, [k1-tbl, p1] 3 times, [ssk] twice, yo, p3, MB, p4; repeat from * to end.
Rnd 14: *[P1, k1-tbl] 3 times, p1, k2, p9; repeat from * to end.
Rnd 15: *Yo, [p1, k1-tbl] 3 times, p1, ssk, p6, k2tog, yo, p1; repeat from * to end.
Rnd 16: *P2, [k1-tbl, p1] 3 times, k1, p6, k1, p2; repeat from * to end.
Rnd 17: *P1, yo, [p1, k1-tbl] 3 times, k2tog, p2, MB, p2, k2tog, p1, yo, p1; repeat from * to end.
Rnd 18: *P3, [k1-tbl, p1] twice, k1-tbl, k1, p5, k1, p3; repeat from * to end.
Rnd 19: *P2, yo, p1, [k1-tbl, p1] twice, k2tog, p4, k2tog, p1, k1-tbl, yo, p1; repeat from * to end.
Rnd 20: *P4, [k1-tbl, p1] twice, k1, p4, k1, p1, k1-tbl, p2; repeat from * to end.
Rnd 21: *P3, yo, [p1, k1-tbl] twice, k2tog, p3, k2tog, p1, k1-tbl, p1, yo, p1; repeat from * to end.
Rnd 22: *P5, k1-tbl, p1, k1-tbl, k1, p3, k1, p1, k1-tbl, p3; repeat from * to end.
Rnd 23: *P4, yo, p1, k1-tbl, p1, k2tog, p2, k2tog, [p1, k1-tbl] twice, yo, p1; repeat from * to end.
Rnd 24: *P6, k1-tbl, p1, k1, p2, k1, [p1, k1-tbl] twice, p2; repeat from * to end.
Rnd 25: *P1, MB, p3, yo, p1, k1-tbl, [k2tog, p1] twice, [k1-tbl, p1] twice, yo, p1; repeat from * to end.

Rnd 26: *P7, k1-tbl, [k1, p1] twice, k1-tbl, p1, k1-tbl, p3; repeat from * to end.
Rnd 27: *P6, yo, p1, [k2tog] twice, [p1, k1-tbl] 3 times, yo, p1; repeat from * to end.
Rnd 28: *P8, k2, [p1, k1-tbl] 3 times, p2; repeat from * to end.
Rnd 29: *P3, MB, p3, yo, k3tog, [p1, k1-tbl] 3 times, p1, yo, p1; repeat from * to end.
Rnd 30: *P8, k1, [p1, k1-tbl] 3 times, p3; repeat from * to end.
Repeat Rnds 1-30 for Pattern B.

PATTERN C
(panel of 4 sts; 4-rnd repeat)
Rnds 1 and 2: K3, p1.
Rnd 3: Pkok, p1.
Rnd 4: Repeat Rnd 1.
Repeat Rnds 1-4 for Pattern C.

LEG

CO 96 sts. Divide sts evenly among 3 needles (32-32-32). Join for working in the rnd, being careful not to twist sts; place marker (pm) for beginning of rnd. Begin Pattern A; work even for 2".

Next Rnd: *P5, work Pattern B over next 18 sts, p5, pm, work Pattern C over next 4 sts, pm; repeat from * to end, omitting last pm. Work even for 19 rnds.

Shape Calf: Decrease 6 sts this rnd, then every 10 rnds 4 times, as follows: *P2tog, work to 2 sts before next marker, p2tog, slip marker (sm), work to next marker, sm; repeat from * to end–66 sts remain. Work even until 4 vertical repeats of Pattern B have been completed. Redistribute sts among 4 needles (16-17-17-16). Remove all markers except for beginning of rnd marker.

HEEL FLAP

Set-Up Row 1 (RS): K16, turn.
Set-Up Row 2: Slip 1, p31, working all 32 sts onto 1 needle for Heel Flap, and removing marker. Leave remaining 34 sts on 2 needles for instep.
Row 1: Working only on 32 Heel Flap sts, *slip 1, k1; repeat from * to end.
Row 2: Slip 1, purl to end.
Repeat Rows 1 and 2 eleven times.

TURN HEEL

Set-Up Row 1 (RS): Slip 1, k17, skp, k1, turn.
Set-Up Row 2: Slip 1, p5, p2tog, p1, turn.
Row 1: Slip 1, knit to 1 st before gap, skp (the 2 sts on either side of gap), k1, turn.
Row 2: Slip 1, purl to 1 st before gap, p2tog (the 2 sts on either side of gap), p1, turn.
Repeat Rows 1 and 2 five times, omitting final k1 and p1 sts in last repeat of Rows 1 and 2–18 sts remain.

GUSSET

Next Row (RS): *Needle 1:* Knit across Heel Flap sts, pick up and knit 13 sts along left side of Heel Flap, M1; *Needle 2:* K1, p1, work 4 sts in Pattern C as established, k11; *Needle 3:* K5, p2tog, work 4 sts in Pattern C as established, k4, k2tog; *Needle 4:* M1, pick up and knit 13 sts along left side of Heel Flap, k9 from Needle 1. Join for working in the rnd; pm for beginning of rnd–78 sts (23-17-15-23). Slip last st on Needle 2 to Needle 3 so that there are 16 sts each on Needles 2 and 3.
Next Rnd: *Needle 1:* Knit to last 2 sts, skp; *Needle 2:* K1, p1, work 4 sts in Pattern C as established, k10; *Needle 3:* K6, p1, work 4 sts in Pattern C as established, k5; *Needle 4:* K2tog, knit to end–76 sts remain.
Decrease Rnd: *Needle 1:* Knit to last 3 sts, skp, k1; *Needles 2 and 3:* Work even as established; *Needle 4:* K1, k2tog, knit to end–74 sts remain (21-16-16-21).
Work even for 1 rnd.
Repeat Decrease Rnd every other rnd 5 times–64 sts remain (16-16-16-16).

FOOT

Work even until Foot measures 3¾" less than desired length from back of Heel.
Next Rnd: Change to St st (knit every rnd) across all sts. *Note: If you prefer, you may continue working pattern as established rather than changing to St st.* Work even until Foot measures 8", or 1½" less than desired length from back of Heel.

TOE

Decrease Rnd: *Needle 1:* Knit to last 3 sts, skp, k1; *Needle 2:* K1, k2tog, knit to end; *Needle 3:* Knit to last 3 sts, skp, k1; *Needle 4:* K1, k2tog, knit to end–60 sts remain. Knit 2 rnds.
Repeat Decrease Rnd every 3 rnds twice, every other rnd 5 times, then every rnd 3 times–20 sts remain (5-5-5-5). Knit to end of Needle 1.

FINISHING

Break yarn, leaving long tail. Transfer sts from Needle 1 to Needle 4, and sts from Needle 3 to Needle 2. Using Kitchener st (see General Techniques, page 140), graft Toe sts. Weave in ends. Block lightly.

japanese
garden

Known for their serene and simple settings, Japanese gardens may include countless elements—bridges, lanterns, paths, ponds, sand and pebbles, shrubs and flowers, streams, waterfalls, stones, and trees—each of which carries a particular purpose or meaning.

I like to think the symmetrical pattern in the Japanese Garden kneesocks also invokes serenity when looked at, although it, like Japanese gardens themselves, is composed of many elements. This pattern is very serene and simple, with "paths" of purl stitches, and plantlike motifs separated by "buds" created with the three-stitch lift. The ribbed triangle on the calf portion of the sock (see page 42), which conceals a decrease, is reminiscent of a small island in the midst of such a garden.

FINISHED MEASUREMENTS
8½" Foot circumference
10½" Foot length from back of Heel
15¼" Leg length to base of Heel, unrolled

YARN
Manos Del Uruguay (100% wool; 100 grams / 138 yards): 3 hanks #X Topaz

NEEDLES
One set of five double-pointed needles (dpn) size US 5 (3.75 mm)
Change needle size if necessary to obtain correct gauge.

NOTIONS
Stitch marker

GAUGE
19 sts and 27 rnds = 4" (10 cm) in Stockinette stitch (St st)

ABBREVIATIONS
3-st lift: Wyib, *insert right-hand needle into st 3 rows below next st on left-hand needle, draw up a loop*, yo; repeat from * to * once; drop st from left-hand needle, allowing it to unravel back to lifted st (see page 15).

STITCH PATTERNS

PATTERN A
(multiple of 2 sts; 1-rnd repeat)
All Rnds: *K1, p1; repeat from * to end.

PATTERN B
(multiple of 10 sts; 20-rnd repeat)
Note: Two sts are increased in each repeat on Rnds 5 and 15; original st count is restored on Rnds 7 and 17.
Rnds 1, 3, and 9: *K2tog, yo, k1, yo, ssk, p5; repeat from * to end.
Rnds 2, 4, 8, and 10: *K5, p5; repeat from * to end.
Rnd 5: *K2tog, yo, k1, yo, ssk, p2, 3-st lift, p2; repeat from * to end.
Rnd 6: *K5, p2, k3, p2; repeat from * to end.
Rnd 7: *K2tog, yo, k1, yo, ssk, p2, s2kp2, p2; repeat from * to end.
Rnds 11, 13, and 19: *P5, k2tog, yo, k1, yo, ssk; repeat from * to end.
Rnds 12, 14, and 18: *P5, k5; repeat from * to end.
Rnd 15: *P2, 3-st lift, p2, k2tog, yo, k1, yo, ssk; repeat from * to end.
Rnd 16: *P2, k3, p2, k5; repeat from * to end.
Rnd 17: *P2, s2kp2, p2, k2tog, yo, k1, yo, ssk; repeat from * to end.
Rnd 20: Repeat Rnd 12.
Repeat Rnds 1-20 for Pattern B.

LEG

CO 60 sts. Divide sts among 4 needles (20-10-10-20). Join for working in the rnd, being careful not to twist sts; place marker (pm) for beginning of rnd. Knit 4 rnds.
Next Rnd: Change to Pattern A; work even until piece measures 1½" from the beginning.
Next Rnd: Work Pattern A over next 10 sts, work Pattern B over next 40 sts, work Pattern A

to end. Work even for 3 rnds.
Shape Calf: Decrease 2 sts this rnd, then every 5 rnds 9 times, as follows: Work 2 sts together, work to last 2 sts, work 2 sts together–40 sts remain (10-10-10-10). *Note: To maintain rib pattern while decreasing, if first 2 sts of rnd are k1, p1, work p2tog; if first 2 sts are p1, k1, work k2tog. If last 2 sts of rnd are k1, p1, work skp; if last 2 sts are p1, k1, work p2tog.* Work even until 3 vertical repeats of Pattern B have been completed. Work Rnds 1-10 of Pattern B once.

HEEL FLAP
Set-Up Row 1 (RS): K10, turn.
Set-Up Row 2: Slip 1, p19, working all 20 sts onto 1 needle for Heel Flap, and removing marker. Leave remaining 20 sts on 2 needles for instep.

Row 1: Working only on 20 Heel Flap sts, *slip 1, k1; repeat from * to end.
Row 2: Slip 1, purl to end.
Repeat Rows 1 and 2 nine times.

TURN HEEL
Set-Up Row 1 (RS): Slip 1, k11, skp, k1, turn.
Set-Up Row 2: Slip 1, p5, p2tog, p1, turn.
Row 1: Slip 1, knit to 1 st before gap, skp (the 2 sts on either side of gap), k1, turn.
Row 2: Slip 1, purl to 1 st before gap, p2tog (the 2 sts on either side of gap), p1, turn.
Repeat Rows 1 and 2 twice, omitting final k1 and p1 in last repeat of Rows 1 and 2–12 sts remain.

GUSSET

Next Row (RS): *Needle 1:* Knit across Heel Flap sts, pick up and knit 11 sts along left side of Heel Flap, M1; *Needles 2 and 3:* Knit across sts on instep needles; *Needle 4:* M1, pick up and knit 11 sts along right side of Heel Flap, k6 from Needle 1. Join for working in the rnd; pm for beginning of rnd–56 sts (18-10-10-18).

Next Rnd: *Needle 1:* Knit to last 2 sts, skp; *Needles 2 and 3:* Knit; *Needle 4:* K2tog, knit to end–54 sts remain.

Decrease Rnd: *Needle 1:* Knit to last 3 sts, skp, k1; *Needles 2 and 3:* Knit; *Needle 4:* K1, k2tog, knit to end–52 sts remain (16-10-10-16). Work even for 1 rnd.

Repeat Decrease Rnd every other rnd 6 times–40 sts remain (10-10-10-10).

FOOT

Work even until Foot measures 9", or 1½" less than desired length from back of Heel.

TOE

Decrease Rnd: *Needle 1:* Knit to last 3 sts, skp, k1; *Needle 2:* K1, k2tog, knit to end; *Needle 3:* Knit to last 3 sts, skp, k1; *Needle 4:* K1, k2tog, knit to end–36 sts remain. Knit 1 rnd.

Repeat Decrease Rnd every other rnd 4 times–20 sts remain (5-5-5-5). Knit to end of Needle 1.

FINISHING

Break yarn, leaving long tail. Transfer sts from Needle 1 to Needle 4, and sts from Needle 3 to Needle 2. Using Kitchener st (see General Techniques, page 140), graft Toe sts. Weave in ends. Block lightly.

KEY

☐ **Knit**

⊡ **Purl**

Ⓞ **Yo**

◩ **K2tog**

◪ **Ssk**

⟑ **S2kp2**

▥ **K3**

▮₃ **3-st lift:** Wyib, *insert right-hand needle into st 3 rows below next st on left-hand needle, draw up a loop*, yo; repeat from * to * once; drop st from left-hand needle, allowing it to unravel back to lifted st (see page 15).

PATTERN B

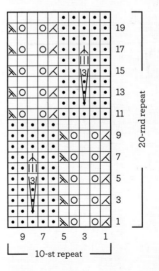

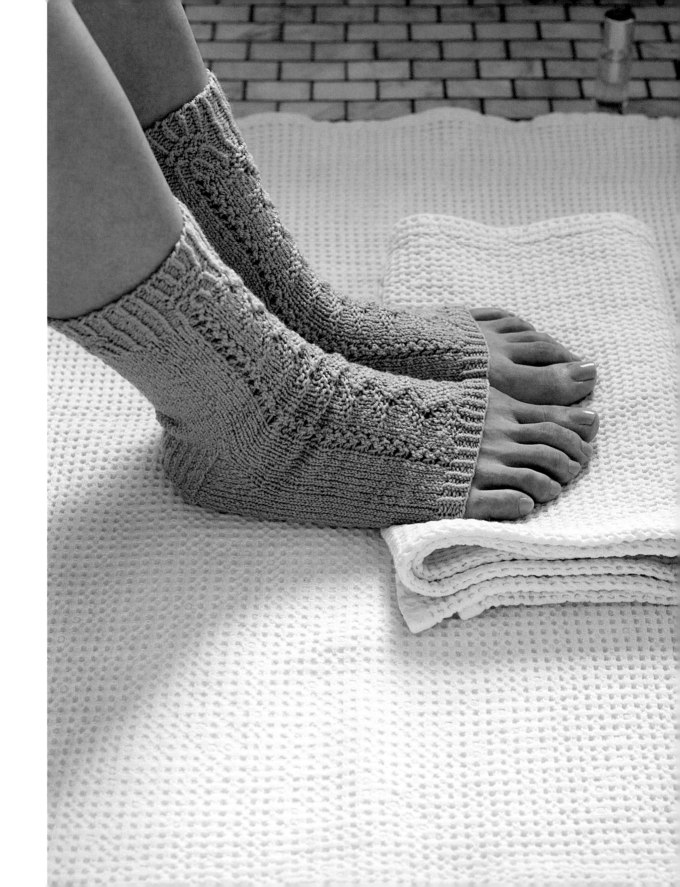

fuji *pedicure*

When I first learned that, in Japanese, *fuji* refers to a very soft silk fabric with a matte finish and an elegant drape, I thought it would be a good name for socks worn during a pedicure, when you're having your feet pampered to silky perfection.

The primary design of this sock is a zigzag lace pattern, reminiscent of small leaves, that runs from the top of the sock down the instep. The rib pattern at the ankle incorporates separate, decorative diamonds made using the pkok embedded within a twisted rib. The sock is designed to stop about an inch before your toes, so that your pedicurist can polish your toenails with your socks on. Then, when she is done, you are able to step into your flip-flops and be on your way without risking any smudging to your polish.

FINISHED MEASUREMENTS
7" Foot circumference
7¼" Foot length from back of Heel
7½" Leg length to base of Heel

YARN
Knit 1, Crochet Too Soxx Appeal (96% superwash merino wool / 3% nylon / 1% elastic; 50 grams / 208 yards): 2 balls #9510 Seafoam

NEEDLES
One set of five double-pointed needles (dpn) size US 2 (2.75 mm)
Change needle size if necessary to obtain correct gauge.

NOTIONS
Stitch marker

GAUGE
29 sts and 49 rnds = 4" (10 cm) in Stockinette stitch (St st)

ABBREVIATIONS
Pkok: Slip third st on left-hand needle over first 2 sts and off needle; k1, yo, k1 (see page 12).

STITCH PATTERNS

PATTERN A
(multiple of 14 sts)

Rnds 1-5: *K1-tbl, p1; repeat from * to end.

Rnds 6 and 14: *[K1-tbl, p1] 3 times, pkok, [p1, k1-tbl] twice, p1; repeat from * to end.

Rnds 7 and 13: *[K1-tbl, p1] 3 times, k3, [p1, k1-tbl] twice, p1; repeat from * to end.

Rnds 8 and 12: *[K1-tbl, p1] twice, pkok, k1, pkok, p1, k1-tbl, p1; repeat from * to end.

Rnds 9 and 11: *[K1-tbl, p1] twice, k7, p1, k1- tbl, p1; repeat from * to end.

Rnd 10: *[K1-tbl, p1] twice, k2, pkok, k2, p1, k1-tbl, p1; repeat from * to end.

Rnds 15-18: Repeat Rnd 1.

PATTERN B
(panel of 16 sts; 12-rnd repeat)

Rnd 1: Yo, ssk, k3, p3, k2tog, yo, k4, yo, ssk.

Rnd 2 and all Even-Numbered Rnds: Knit.

Rnd 3: K2tog, yo, k2, p3, k2tog, yo, k5, k2tog, yo.

Rnd 5: Yo, ssk, k1, p3, k2tog, yo, k6, yo, ssk.

Rnd 7: K2tog, yo, k4, yo, ssk, p3, k3, k2tog, yo.

Rnd 9: Yo, ssk, k5, yo, ssk, p3, k2, yo, ssk.

Rnd 11: K2tog, yo, k6, yo, ssk, p3, k1, k2tog, yo.

Rnd 12: Knit.

Repeat Rnds 1-12 for Pattern B.

LEG

CO 56 sts. Divide sts evenly among 4 needles (14-14-14-14). Join for working in the rnd, being careful not to twist sts; place marker (pm) for beginning of rnd. Begin Pattern A; work even for 18 rnds.

Next Rnd: Slip sts from Needle 3 onto Needle 2 (14-28-14). ***Needle 1:*** Knit; ***Needle 2:*** K6, pm, work Pattern B across 16 sts, pm, k6; ***Needle 3:*** Knit. Work even until 4 vertical repeats of Pattern B have been completed.

HEEL FLAP

Set-Up Row 1 (RS): K14, turn.

Set-Up Row 2: Slip 1, p27, working all 28 sts onto 1 needle for Heel Flap, and removing marker. Leave remaining 28 sts on 1 needle for instep.

Row 1: Working only on 28 Heel Flap sts, *slip 1, k1; repeat from * to end.

Row 2: Slip 1, purl to end.

Repeat Rows 1 and 2 eleven times.

TURN HEEL

Set-Up Row 1 (RS): Slip 1, k15, skp, k1, turn.

Set-Up Row 2: Slip 1, p5, p2tog, p1, turn.

Row 1: Slip 1, knit to 1 st before gap, skp (the 2 sts on either side of gap), k1, turn.

Row 2: Slip 1, purl to 1 st before gap, p2tog (the 2 sts on either side of gap), p1, turn.

Repeat Rows 1 and 2 four times, omitting final k1 and p1 sts in last repeat of Rows 1 and 2–16 sts remain.

GUSSET

Next Row (RS): *Needle 1:* Knit across Heel Flap sts, pick up and knit 13 sts along left side of Heel Flap, M1; *Needle 2:* Continue pattern as established across instep needles; *Needle 3:* M1, pick up and knit 13 sts along right side of Heel Flap, k8 from Needle 1. Join for working in the rnd; pm for beginning of rnd–72 sts (22-28-22).

Next Rnd: *Needle 1:* Knit to last 2 sts, skp; *Needle 2:* Work even; *Needle 3:* K2tog, knit to end–70 sts remain.

Decrease Rnd: *Needle 1:* Knit to last 3 sts, skp, k1; *Needle 2:* Work even; *Needle 3:* K1, k2tog, knit to end–68 sts remain (20-28-20). Work even for 1 rnd.

Repeat Decrease Rnd every other rnd 6 times–56 sts remain (14-28-14).

FOOT

Work even until Foot measures 4¾", or 2½" less than desired length from back of Heel, or to 1" before the base of your toes.

Next Rnd: Change to Pattern A; work Rnd 1 six times. BO all sts loosely in pattern.

Weave in ends. Block lightly.

KEY

☐ Knit

⊡ Purl

Ⓠ K1-tbl

Ⓞ Yo

◩ K2tog

◪ Ssk

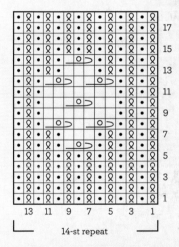

Pkok: Slip third st on left-hand needle over first 2 sts and off needle; k1, yo, k1 (see page 12).

PATTERN A

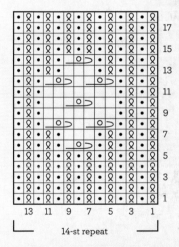

14-st repeat

PATTERN B

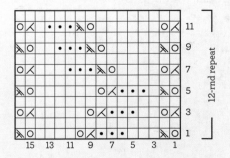

12-rnd repeat

~ **47**

shiatsu

Shiatsu is a Japanese form of massage that uses finger pressure much like acupuncture to open the natural flow of energy through the body. The practitioner uses finger and palm pressure to stimulate the flow of this energy, called *qi* (pronounced "chee"). Scientists believe that shiatsu calms an overactive sympathetic nervous system to improve circulation, relieve stiff muscles, and alleviate stress.

I began the leg with a complex design that ultimately ends with many wrapped stitches. From this top, which can be folded over when worn, the body flows into a very simple stitch pattern that incorporates the pkok and appears to be a cable that has become untangled, like nerves that have relaxed during a shiatsu massage. The sock ends in a stirrup rather than a full foot so that it can be worn with sandals or easily layered with other footwear inside a boot.

FINISHED MEASUREMENTS

10" Leg circumference, at widest point
7½" Leg circumference, at narrowest point
15" Leg length, with Cuff folded down

YARN

Lorna's Laces Green Line DK
(100% organic merino wool; 2 ounces /
145 yards): 2 hanks #3812 Solitude

NEEDLES

One 16" (40 cm) circular (circ) needle size US 5 (3.75 mm)
One set of five double-pointed needles (dpn) size US 4 (3.5 mm)
Change needle size if necessary to obtain correct gauge.

NOTIONS

Stitch marker; stitch holder; cable needle (cn)

GAUGE

24 sts and 31 rnds = 4" (10 cm) in Stockinette stitch (St st), using smaller needles

ABBREVIATIONS

Pkok: Slip third st on left-hand needle over first 2 sts and off needle; k1, yo, k1 (see page 12).
Wrap14: Slip next 14 sts to cn, wrap yarn counterclockwise around base of sts 3 times, work the wrapped sts k1, [ssk, k2tog] 3 times, k1 (see page 13)—6 sts decreased.

KEY

☐	**Knit**
⊡	**Purl**
☒	**K1-tbl**
⊏⊙⊐	**Pkok:** Slip third st on left-hand needle over first 2 sts and off needle; k1, yo, k1 (see page 12).

PATTERN C

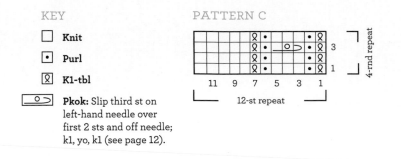

STITCH PATTERNS

PATTERN A
(multiple of 22 sts at CO; multiple varies)
Rnds 1 and 2: Knit.
Rnd 3: Purl.
Rnds 4 and 5: *K2, p2, [k4, p2] 3 times; repeat from * to end.
Rnd 6: *K2, yo, p2, [k4, p2] 3 times, yo; repeat from * to end–24 sts.
Rnd 7: *K3, p2, [k4, p2] 3 times, p1; repeat from * to end.
Rnd 8: *K3, yo, p2, [k4, p2] 3 times, yo, k1; repeat from * to end–26 sts.
Rnd 9: *[K4, p2] 4 times, k2; repeat from * to end.
Rnd 10: *K4, yo, p2, [k4, p2] 3 times, yo, k2; repeat from * to end–28 sts.
Rnd 11: *K5, p2, [k4, p2] 3 times, k3; repeat from * to end.
Rnd 12:*K2, yo, k2tog, k1, yo, p2, [k4, p2] 3 times, yo, k1, k2tog, yo; repeat from * to end– 30 sts.
Rnd 13: *K6, p2, [k4, p2] 3 times, k4; repeat from * to end.
Rnd 14: *K3, yo, k2tog, k1, yo, p1, p2tog, k2, ssp, p1, k4, p1, p2tog, k2, ssp, p1, yo, k1, k2tog, yo, k1–28 sts remain.
Rnd 15: *K7, p2, k2, p2, k4, p2, k2, p2, k5; repeat from * to end.

Rnd 16: *K4, yo, k2tog, k1, yo, p2, k2, p1, p2tog, k2, ssp, p1, k2, p2, yo, k1, k2tog, yo, k2; repeat from * to end.
Rnd 17: *K8, p2, [k2, p2] 3 times, k6; repeat from * to end.
Rnd 18: *K5, yo, k2tog, k1, wrap 14, k1, k2tog, yo, k3; repeat from * to end–22 sts remain.
Rnd 19: Purl.
Rnd 20: *P7, ssp, p6, p2tog, p5; repeat from * to end–20 sts remain.
Rnd 21: Knit.

PATTERN B
(multiple of 2 sts; 1-rnd/ row repeat)
All Rnds/Rows: *K1, p1; repeat from * to end.

PATTERN C
(multiple of 12 sts; 4-rnd repeat)
Rnds 1 and 2: *K1-tbl, p1, k3, p1, k1-tbl, k5; repeat from * to end.
Rnd 3: *K1-tbl, p1, pkok, p1, k1-tbl, k5; repeat from * to end.
Rnd 4: Repeat Rnd 1.
Repeat Rnds 1-4 for Pattern B.

PATTERN D
(multiple of 4 sts; 1-rnd repeat)
All Rnds: *K2, p2; repeat from * to end.

CUFF

Using circ needle, CO 66 sts. Join for working in the rnd, being careful not to twist sts; place marker (pm) for beginning of rnd. Begin Pattern A; work even for 21 rnds, working decreases as indicated in Pattern– 60 sts remain. *Note: Cuffs are reversible and can be worn as shown or folded over.*

LEG

Note: Change to dpn when necessary for number of sts on needle.
Next Rnd: Change to Pattern B; work even for 8 rnds.
Next Rnd: Change to Pattern C; work even for 8 rnds.
Decrease Rnd: Decrease 2 sts this rnd, then every 8 rnds 5 times, as follows: Work 2 together, work to last 2 sts, work 2 together–48 sts remain. *Note: To maintain pattern while decreasing, if second st of rnd is a knit st, work k2tog; if second st is a purl st, work p2tog. If next-to-last st of rnd is a knit st, work skp; if next-to-last st is a purl st, work p2tog. If you are unable to work a complete pkok on Rnd 3, work remaining sts in St st.* Work even until piece measures 16" from the beginning.
Next Rnd: Change to Pattern D. Work even for 1½".

STIRRUP

Next Rnd: K15, BO next 18 sts, k6 and place on holder for right side of Stirrup, BO next 18 sts, k6 for left side of Stirrup–6 sts remain.
Next Row (WS): Working back and forth on 6 Stirrup sts, begin Pattern B; work even until Stirrup measures 7". Using 3-Needle BO or Kitchener st (see General Techniques, pages 140 and 141), graft to Stirrup sts on holder.
Weave in ends. Block lightly.

haiku

The Sock

Sock on the needles
Naked foot in its future
Warm and beautiful

Haiku is a form of non-rhyming Japanese poetry in which simple words are used to "paint" an image in the mind of the reader. Among the most common themes are nature and the poet's feelings and life experiences. Often in haiku, there are five syllables in the first line, seven in the second line, and five in the third, for a total of seventeen syllables overall. The challenge of haiku is to express the poem's meaning and imagery in this sparse, strict format. While these poems seem very simple, they are often quite difficult to construct.

A sock itself could be compared to a haiku—a limited design area with a specific format, on which a knitter strives to convey something that is at once original, functional, and beautiful. These socks, in particular, mirror this type of poetry with their relatively simple, yet strangely complex stitch pattern, which includes a three-stitch lift maneuver that yields a lovely knot in the midst of a lace panel. It may seem complicated when you first try it, but it becomes easier after just a little practice. These socks even inspired me to write the haiku at the top of the page.

FINISHED MEASUREMENTS
7½" Foot circumference
10" Foot length from back of Heel
7½" Leg length to base of Heel

YARN
Jojoland Melody Superwash (100% superwash wool; 50 grams / 220 yards): 2 balls #MS14

NOTIONS
Stitch marker

NEEDLES
One set of five double-pointed needles (dpn) size US 1 (2.25 mm)
Change needle size if necessary to obtain correct gauge.

GAUGE
30 sts and 40 rnds = 4" (10 cm) in Stockinette stitch (St st)

ABBREVIATIONS
3-st lift: Wyib, *insert right-hand needle into st 3 rows below next st on left-hand needle, draw up a loop*, yo; repeat from * to * once; drop st from left-hand needle, allowing it to unravel back to lifted st (see page 15).

KEY

- **·**   Purl
- **Ⴘ**   K1-tbl
- **O**   Yo
- **⊠**   P2tog
- **⊠**   P2tog-tbl
- **Ⴊ**   S2kp2
- **⫼**   K3
- **⟨3⟩**   **3-st lift:** Wyib, *insert right-hand needle into st 3 rows below next st on left-hand needle, draw up a loop*, yo; repeat from * to * once; drop st from left-hand needle, allowing it to unravel back to lifted st (see page 15).

PATTERN B

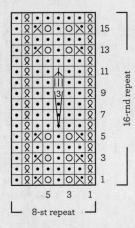

16-rnd repeat

5   3   1

8-st repeat

STITCH PATTERNS

PATTERN A
(multiple of 2 sts; 1-rnd repeat)
All Rnds: *K1-tbl, p1; repeat from * to end.

PATTERN B
(multiple of 8 sts; 16-rnd repeat)
Note: Two sts are increased in each repeat on Rnd 9; original st count is restored on Rnd 11.
Rnds 1, 3, 5, 13, and 15: *K1-tbl, p2tog-tbl, yo, p1, yo, p2tog, k1-tbl, p1; repeat from * to end.
Rnds 2, 4, 6-8, 12, and 14: *K1-tbl, p5, k1-tbl, p1; repeat from * to end.
Rnd 9: *K1-tbl, p2, 3-st lift, p2, k1-tbl, p1; repeat from * to end.
Rnd 10: *K1-tbl, p2, k3, p2, k1-tbl, p1; repeat from * to end.
Rnd 11: *K1-tbl, p2, s2kp2, p2, k1-tbl, p1; repeat from * to end.
Rnd 16: Repeat Rnd 2.
Repeat Rnds 1-16 for Pattern B.

LEG
CO 64 sts. Divide sts evenly among 4 needles (16-16-16-16). Join for working in the rnd, being careful not to twist sts; place marker (pm) for beginning of rnd. Begin Pattern A; work even for 1½".
Next Rnd: Change to Pattern B; work even until 3 vertical repeats of Pattern B have been completed.

HEEL FLAP
Set-Up Row 1 (RS): K16, turn.
Set-Up Row 2: Slip 1, p31, working all 32 sts onto 1 needle for Heel Flap, and removing marker. Leave remaining 32 sts on 2 needles for instep.
Row 1 (RS): Working only on 32 Heel Flap sts, *slip 1, k1; repeat from * to end.
Row 2: Slip 1, purl to end.
Repeat Rows 1 and 2 eleven times.

TURN HEEL

Set-Up Row 1: Slip 1, k17, skp, k1, turn.

Set-Up Row 2: Slip 1, p5, p2tog, p1, turn.

Row 1: Slip 1, knit to 1 st before gap, skp (the 2 sts on either side of gap), k1, turn.

Row 2: Slip 1, purl to 1 st before gap, p2tog (the 2 sts on either side of gap), p1, turn.

Repeat Rows 1 and 2 five times, omitting final k1 and p1 sts in last repeat of Rows 1 and 2–18 sts remain.

GUSSET

Next Rnd (RS): *Needle 1:* Knit across Heel Flap sts, pick up and knit 13 sts along left side of Heel Flap, M1; *Needles 2 and 3:* Continue Pattern B as established; *Needle 4:* M1, pick up and knit 13 sts along right side of Heel Flap, k9 from Needle 1. Join for working in the rnd; pm for beginning of rnd–78 sts (23-16-16-23).

Next Rnd: *Needle 1:* Knit to last 2 sts, skp; *Needles 2 and 3:* Work even as established; *Needle 4:* K2tog, knit to end–76 sts remain.

Decrease Rnd: *Needle 1:* Knit to last 3 sts, skp, k1; *Needles 2 and 3:* Work even as established; *Needle 4:* K1, k2tog, knit to end–74 sts remain (21-16-16-21). Work even for 1 rnd.

Repeat Decrease Rnd every other rnd 5 times–64 sts remain (16-16-16-16).

FOOT

Work even until Foot measures 8½", or 1½" less than desired length from back of Heel.

Note: Do not end with Rnd 9 or 10 of Pattern B.

TOE

Decrease Rnd: *Needle 1:* Knit to last 3 sts, skp, k1; *Needle 2:* K1, k2tog, knit to end; *Needle 3:* Knit to last 3 sts, skp, k1; *Needle 4:* K1, k2tog, knit to end–60 sts remain. Knit 1 rnd.

Repeat Decrease Rnd every other rnd ten times–20 sts remain (5-5-5-5). Knit to end of Needle 1.

FINISHING

Break yarn, leaving long tail. Transfer sts from Needle 1 to Needle 4, and sts from Needle 3 to Needle 2. Using Kitchener st (see General Techniques, page 140), graft Toe sts. Weave in ends. Block lightly.

japanese fan tabi

Fans are a traditional element of Japanese costume, their history stretching back thousands of years. They were not only used as a way to cool oneself, but were also considered status symbols, ceremonial devices, and an ornamental part of one's appearance. Many versions of these fans are still made today, and display amazingly decorative artwork. I've paired the fan theme here with a traditional Japanese *tabi* sock, which has a separate big toe so it can be worn with flip-flops or thong sandals.

The Japanese Fan Tabi socks earned their name when I saw the pattern that included a portion of our familiar feather and fan pattern—the difference here is that a triple decrease narrows the portion of the design that is usually taken up by many single decreases. The scalloped seed stitch edging further underscores the fan theme.

FINISHED MEASUREMENTS
8" Foot circumference
9½" Foot length from back of Heel
7¼" Leg length to base of Heel

YARN
ShibuiKnits Sock (100% superwash merino wool; 50 grams / 191 yards):
2 hanks #S1797 Chinese Red

NEEDLES
One set of five double-pointed needles (dpn) size US 1 (2.25 mm)
Change needle size if necessary to obtain correct gauge.

NOTIONS
Stitch marker; stitch holder

GAUGE
31 sts and 44 rnds = 4" (10 cm) in Stockinette stitch (St st)

ABBREVIATIONS
R3D (right-slanting 3-st decrease):
[K2tog] twice, slip these sts back to left-hand needle, pass second st over first st and off needle, slip remaining st back to right-hand needle. *Note: If you prefer, you may work k4tog.*
L3D (left-slanting 3-st decrease):
Ssk, k2tog, pass second st on right-hand needle over last st and off needle.
Note: If you prefer, you may work s3kp3.

STITCH PATTERNS

PATTERN A
(multiple of 2 sts; 1-rnd repeat)

Rnd 1: *K1, p1; repeat from * to end.

Rnd 2: Purl the knit sts and knit the purl sts as they face you.
Repeat Rnd 2 for Pattern A.

PATTERN B
(multiple of 15 sts; 18-rnd repeat)

Rnds 1, 5, and 9: *R3D, [yo, k1] 5 times, yo, L3D, p2; repeat from * to end.

Rnds 2-4, 6-8, 11, and 16: *K13, p2; repeat from * to end.

Rnds 10 and 17: Purl.

Rnds 12 and 14: *[P1, k1] 6 times, p3; repeat from * to end.

Rnds 13 and 15: *[K1, p1] 6 times, k1, p2; repeat from * to end.

Rnd 18: Repeat Rnd 2.
Repeat Rnds 1-18 for Pattern B.

LEG

CO 60 sts. Divide sts evenly among 4 needles (15-15-15-15). Join for working in the rnd, being careful not to twist sts; place marker (pm) for beginning of rnd. Begin Pattern A; work even until piece measures 1" from the beginning.

Next Rnd: Change to Pattern B. Work even until 4 vertical repeats of Pattern B have been completed.

HEEL FLAP

Set-Up Row 1 (RS): K15, turn.

Set-Up Row 2: Slip 1, p29, working all 30 sts onto 1 needle for Heel Flap, and removing marker. Leave remaining 30 sts on 2 needles for instep.

Row 1: Working only on 30 Heel Flap sts, *slip 1, k1; repeat from * to end.

Row 2: Slip 1, purl to end.
Repeat Rows 1 and 2 eleven times.

TURN HEEL

Set-Up Row 1 (RS): Slip 1, k16, skp, k1, turn.

Set-Up Row 2: Slip 1, p5, p2tog, p1, turn.

Row 1: Slip 1, knit to 1 st before gap, skp (the 2 sts on either side of gap), k1, turn.

Row 2: Slip 1, purl to 1 st before gap, p2tog (the 2 sts on either side of gap), p1, turn.
Repeat Rows 1 and 2 four times–18 sts remain.

GUSSET

Next Row (RS): *Needle 1:* Knit across Heel Flap sts, pick up and knit 13 sts along left side of Heel Flap, M1; *Needles 2 and 3:* Work Pattern B as established; *Needle 4:* M1, pick up and knit 13 sts along right side of Heel Flap, k8 from Needle 1. Join for working in the rnd; pm for beginning of rnd–78 sts (23-16-16-23).

Next Rnd: *Needle 1:* Knit to last 2 sts, skp; *Needles 2 and 3:* Work even as established; *Needle 4:* K2tog, knit to end–76 sts remain.

Decrease Rnd: *Needle 1:* Knit to last 3 sts, skp, k1; *Needles 2 and 3:* Work even as established; *Needle 4:* K1, k2tog, knit to end–74 sts remain (21-16-16-21). Work even for 1 rnd. Repeat Decrease Rnd every other rnd 5 times–64 sts remain (16-16-16-16).

FOOT

Work even until Foot measures 8", or 1½" less than desired length from back of Heel.

TABI TOE
RIGHT FOOT
Multi-Toe

Next Rnd: *Needle 1:* Knit to last 3 sts, skp, knit 1; *Needle 2:* K1, k2tog, knit to end; *Needle 3:* K5, transfer remaining 10 sts to st holder, CO 4 sts, k5 from Needle 4; transfer remaining 10 sts from Needle 4 to st holder–44 sts remain (15-15-14).

Decrease Rnd: *Needle 1:* Knit to last 3 sts, skp, k1; *Needle 2:* K1, k2tog, knit to end; *Needle 3:* Knit–42 sts remain (14-14-14). Work even for 1 rnd.

Repeat Decrease Rnd every other rnd 6 times–30 sts remain (8-8-14).

Next Rnd: *Needle 1:* Knit to last 4 sts, [k2tog] twice; *Needle 2:* [Ssk] twice, knit to end; working next 7 sts from Needle 3 onto Needle 2, k3, [k2tog] twice; *Needle 3:* K3, [k2tog] twice, k6 from Needle 1–22 sts remain (11-11). Knit 1 rnd. Using Kitchener st (see General Techniques, page 140), graft sts.

Big Toe

Needle 4: Pick up and knit 6 sts from 4 sts CO between Toes; *Needle 2:* K10 from st holder; *Needle 3:* K10 from st holder–26 sts (6-10-10). Join for working in the rnd; pm for beginning of rnd.

Next Rnd: *Needle 1:* K2tog, k2, k2tog; *Needles 2 and 3:* Work even–24 sts (4-10-10). Work even until Big Toe is approximately ¼" longer than Multi-Toe.

Next Rnd: *K2tog; repeat from * to end–12 sts remain. Break yarn, thread through remaining sts twice, pull tight and fasten off, leaving tail to WS.

LEFT FOOT

Multi-Toe

Knit across Needles 1 and 2. Reposition marker. Renumber needles so that what was previously Needle 3 is now Needle 1. Work Multi-Toe as for Right Foot.

Big Toe

Work as for Right Foot.

FINISHING

Weave in ends. Block lightly.

KEY

☐ Knit

⊡ Purl

⊙ Yo

▨ **R3D (right-slanting 3-st decrease):** [K2tog] twice, slip these sts back to left-hand needle, pass second st over first st and off needle, slip remaining st back to right-hand needle.
Note: If you prefer, you may work k4tog.

▨ **L3D (left-slanting 3-st decrease):** Ssk, k2tog, pass second st on right-hand needle over last st and off needle.
Note: If you prefer, you may work s3kp3.

PATTERN B

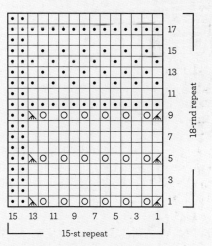

bonsai

Bonsai is the ancient art of dwarfing trees by confining them in containers and carefully pruning them, resulting in a piece of art that entwines man, nature, elements, and change—"heaven and earth in one container," as bonsai is sometimes described. Brought to Japan from China by Buddhist monks in about the twelfth century, bonsai has since become a hobby popular in the Western world as well.

With the Bonsai socks, I attempted to re-create the feel of a decorative tree. The lace leaves are made with centered double decreases and pkoks connect the leaves in a lacy chain. Instead of a typical knit 2, purl 2 ribbing, the pattern extends into the top of the sock for a seamless, decorative ribbing. The pattern has only a ten-stitch repeat but a longer thirty-two-round repeat, and it requires moving one stitch at the end of a round in order to do the two-stitch decrease within the pattern.

FINISHED MEASUREMENTS
7½" Foot circumference
9½" Foot length from back of Heel
9½" Leg length to base of Heel

YARN
Cherry Tree Hill Yarn Supersock Solids (100% merino wool; 4 ounces / 420 yards); 1 hank Loden

NEEDLES
One set of five double-pointed needles (dpn) size 1 (2.25 mm)
Change needle size if necessary to obtain correct gauge.

NOTIONS
Stitch marker

GAUGE
29 sts and 46 rnds = 4" (10 cm) in Stockinette stitch (St st)

ABBREVIATIONS
Pkok: Slip third st on left-hand needle over first 2 sts and off needle; k1, yo, k1 (see page 12).

KEY

☐	Knit
⊡	Purl
⊠	K1-tbl
Ⓞ	Yo
◿	K2tog
◺	Ssk
◺	Sk2p

⬚ Pkok: Slip third st on left-hand needle over first 2 sts and off needle; k1, yo, k1 (see page 12).

PATTERN A

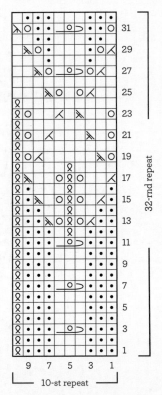

9 7 5 3 1

10-st repeat

32-rnd repeat

PATTERN B

19 17 15 13 11 9 7 5 3 1

4-rnd repeat

STITCH PATTERNS

PATTERN A
(multiple of 10 sts; 32-rnd repeat)

Rnds 1, 2, 4-6, and 8-10: *P3, k3, p3, k1-tbl; repeat from * to end.

Rnds 3, 7, and 11: *P3, pkok, p3, k1-tbl; repeat from * to end.

Rnd 12: *P3, k1, k1-tbl, k1, p3, k1-tbl; repeat from * to end.

Rnd 13: *P2, k2tog, yo, k1-tbl, yo, ssk, p2, k1-tbl; repeat from * to end.

Rnd 14: *P2, k2, k1-tbl, k2, p2, k1-tbl; repeat from * to end.

Rnd 15: *P1, k2tog, k1, yo, k1-tbl, yo, k1, ssk, p1, k1-tbl; repeat from * to end.

Rnd 16: *P1, k3, k1-tbl, k3, p1, k1-tbl; repeat from * to end.

Rnd 17: *K2tog, k2, yo, k1-tbl, yo, k2, ssk, k1-tbl; repeat from * to end.

Rnd 18: *[K4, k1-tbl] twice; repeat from * to end.

Rnd 19: *Yo, ssk, k5, k2tog, yo, k1-tbl; repeat from * to end.

Rnds 20, 22, and 24: *K9, k1-tbl; repeat from *to end.

Rnd 21: *Yo, k1, ssk, k3, k2tog, k1, yo, k1-tbl; repeat from * to end.

Rnd 23: *Yo, k2, ssk, k1, k2tog, k2, yo, k1-tbl; repeat from * to end.

Rnd 25: *K2, k2tog, yo, k1, yo, ssk, k3; repeat from * to end.

Rnd 26: Knit.

Rnd 27: *K1, k2tog, yo, pkok, yo, ssk, k2; repeat from * to end.

Rnd 28: *K2, [p1, k3] twice; repeat from * to end.

Rnd 29: *K2tog, yo, p1, k3, p1, yo, ssk, k1; repeat from * to end.

Rnd 30: *K1, p2, k3, p2, k2; repeat from * to end, move first st of each needle to end of previous needle.

Rnd 31: *Yo, p2, pkok, p2, yo, sk2p; repeat from * to end.

Rnd 32: *P3, k3, p3, k1; repeat from * to end.

Repeat Rnds 1-32 for Pattern A.

PATTERN B
(panel of 19 sts)

Rnds 1 and 2: *P3, k3, p3*, k1-tbl; repeat from * to * once.

Rnd 3: *P3, pkok, p3*, k1-tbl; repeat from * to * once.

Rnd 4: Repeat Rnd 1.

Repeat Rnds 1-4 for Pattern B.

LEG

CO 60 sts. Divide sts evenly among 3 needles (20-20-20). Join for working in the rnd, being careful not to twist sts; place marker (pm) for beginning of rnd. Begin Pattern A; work even until 3 vertical repeats of Pattern A have been completed. Redistribute sts evenly among 4 needles (15-15-15-15). Knit 1 rnd.

HEEL FLAP

Set-Up Row 1 (RS): K15, turn.

Set-Up Row 2: Slip 1, p29, working all 30 sts onto 1 needle for Heel Flap, and removing marker.

Transfer remaining 30 sts to 2 needles (15-15) for instep.

Row 1: Working only on 30 Heel Flap sts, *slip 1, k1; repeat from * to end.

Row 2: Slip 1, purl to end.

Repeat Rows 1 and 2 eleven times.

TURN HEEL

Set-Up Row 1 (RS): Slip 1, k16, skp, k1, turn.

Set-Up Row 2: Slip 1, p5, p2tog, p1, turn.

Row 1: Slip 1, knit to 1 st before gap, skp (the 2 sts on either side of gap), k1, turn.

Row 2: Slip 1, purl to 1 st before gap, p2tog (the 2 sts on either side of gap), p1, turn.

Repeat Rows 1 and 2 four times—18 sts remain.

GUSSET

Next Row (RS): *Needle 1:* Knit across Heel Flap sts, pick up and knit 13 sts along left side of Heel Flap, M1; *Needles 2 and 3:* K5, work Pattern B across next 19 sts, k6; *Needle 4:* M1, pick up and knit 13 sts along right side of heel flap, k8 from Needle 1. Join for working in the rnd; pm for beginning of rnd—76 sts (23-15-15-23).

Next Rnd: *Needle 1:* Knit to last 2 sts, skp; *Needles 2 and 3:* Work even as established; *Needle 4:* K2tog, knit to end—74 sts remain.

Decrease Rnd: *Needle 1:* Knit to last 3 sts, skp, k1; *Needles 2 and 3:* Work even as established; *Needle 4:* K1, k2tog, knit to end—72 sts remain (21-15-15-21). Work even for 1 rnd.

Repeat Decrease Rnd every other rnd 6 times—60 sts remain (15-15-15-15).

FOOT

Work even until Foot measures 8", or 1½" less than desired length from back of Heel.

Next Rnd: Change to St st (knit every rnd) across all sts.

TOE

Decrease Rnd: *Needle 1:* Knit to last 3 sts, skp, k1; *Needle 2:* K1, k2tog, knit to end; *Needle 3:* Knit to last 3 sts, skp, k1; *Needle 4:* K1, k2tog, knit to end—56 sts remain. Knit 1 rnd.

Repeat Decrease Rnd every other rnd 9 times—20 sts remain (5-5-5-5). Knit to end of Needle 1.

FINISHING

Break yarn, leaving long tail. Transfer sts from Needle 1 to Needle 4, and sts from Needle 3 to Needle 2. Using Kitchener st (see General Techniques, page 140), graft Toe sts. Weave in ends. Block lightly.

geisha
lounge

A geisha, which means "person of the arts," is a traditional, female Japanese entertainer, skilled in conversation, tea ceremony, classical music, and dance. True geisha wear elaborate hairstyles, makeup applied in accordance with their age and level of experience, and ornate clothing so layered and complicated that dressing requires professional assistance and might take over an hour. Many years of training are required before being allowed into the "flower and willow world," as the domain of a geisha is sometimes called.

I like to think that these simple but decorative socks also have a place in the "flower and willow world," something a hardworking woman—geisha included— could slip into at the end of a long day or after a relaxing bath. Although they are shorter socks with a plain foot, the pattern in the ribbed top—which extends into the heel flap (see page 66)—adds delicate ornamentation. The pattern is only a six-stitch repeat, but it includes the three-stitch lift, the centered double decrease, and lacework.

FINISHED MEASUREMENTS
7¾" Foot circumference
9½" Foot length from back of Heel
3½" Leg length to base of Heel

YARN
Debbie Bliss Baby Cashmerino (55% merino wool / 33% microfiber / 12% cashmere; 50 grams / 137 yards): 2 balls #10 Lilac

NEEDLES
One set of five double-pointed needles (dpn) size US 2 (2.75 mm)
Change needle size if necessary to obtain correct gauge.

NOTIONS
Stitch marker

GAUGE
25 sts and 35 rnds = 4" (10 cm) in Stockinette stitch (St st)

ABBREVIATIONS
3-st lift: Wyib, *insert right-hand needle into st 3 rows below next st on left-hand needle, draw up a loop*, yo; repeat from * to * once; drop st from left-hand needle, allowing it to unravel back to lifted st (see page 15).

STITCH PATTERNS

PATTERN A IN-THE-RND
(multiple of 6 sts)

Note: Two sts are increased in each repeat on Rnd 9; original st count is restored on Rnd 11.

Rnds 1-4, 6-8, and 12: *K1-tbl, p3, k1-tbl, p1; repeat from * to end.

Rnds 5 and 13: *Skp, yo, p1, yo, k2tog, p1; repeat from * to end.

Rnd 9: *K1-tbl, p1, 3-st lift, p1, k1-tbl, p1; repeat from * to end.

Rnd 10: *K1-tbl, p1, k3, p1, k1-tbl, p1; repeat from * to end.

Rnd 11: *K1-tbl, p1, s2kp2, p1, k1-tbl, p1; repeat from * to end.

Rnds 14-16: Repeat Rnd 1.

PATTERN A BACK-AND-FORTH
(multiple of 6 sts)

Note: Two sts are increased in each repeat on Row 9; original st count is restored on Row 11.

Rows 1, 3, 7, and 15 (RS): *K1-tbl, p3, k1-tbl, p1; repeat from * to end.

Rows 2, 4, 6, 8, 12, and 14: *K1, p1-tbl, k3, p1-tbl; repeat from * to end.

Rows 5 and 13: *Skp, yo, p1, yo, k2tog, p1; repeat from * to end.

Row 9: *K1-tbl, p1, 3-st lift, p1, k1-tbl, p1; repeat from * to end.

Row 10: *K1, p1-tbl, k1, p3, k1, p1-tbl; repeat from * to end.

Row 11: *K1-tbl, p1, s2kp2, p1, k1-tbl, p1; repeat from * to end.

Row 16: Repeat Row 2.

LEG

CO 48 sts. Divide sts evenly among 4 needles (12-12-12-12). Join for working in the rnd, being careful not to twist sts; place marker (pm) for beginning of rnd. Begin Pattern A In-the-Rnd; work even for 16 rnds.

HEEL FLAP

Set-Up Row 1 (RS): Change to Pattern A Back-and-Forth; work across Needle 1, turn.

Row 1: Work across Needles 1 and 4, working all 24 sts onto 1 needle for Heel Flap, and removing marker. Leave remaining 24 sts on 2 needles for instep. Working only on 24 Heel Flap sts, work even until 1 vertical repeat of Pattern A Back-and-Forth is complete.

TURN HEEL

Set-Up Row 1 (RS): Slip 1, k13, skp, k1, turn.

Set-Up Row 2: Slip 1, p5, p2tog, p1, turn.

Row 1: Slip 1, knit to 1 st before gap, skp (the 2 sts on either side of gap), k1, turn.

Row 2: Slip 1, purl to 1 st before gap, p2tog (the 2 sts on either side of gap), p1, turn.

Repeat Rows 1 and 2 three times, omitting final k1 and p1 sts in last repeat of Rows 1 and 2–14 sts remain.

GUSSET

Next Row (RS): *Needle 1:* Knit across Heel Flap sts, pick up and knit 12 sts along left side of Heel Flap, M1; *Needles 2 and 3:* Knit across sts on instep needles; *Needle 4:* M1, pick up and knit 12 sts along right side of Heel Flap, k7 from Needle 1. Join for working in the rnd; pm for beginning of rnd–64 sts (20-12-12-20).

Next Rnd: *Needle 1:* Knit to last 2 sts, skp; *Needles 2 and 3:* Knit; *Needle 4:* K2tog, knit to end–62 sts remain.

Decrease Rnd: *Needle 1:* Knit to last 3 sts, skp, k1; *Needles 2 and 3:* Knit; *Needle 4:* K1, k2tog, knit to end–60 sts remain (18-12-12-18). Work even for 1 rnd.

Repeat Decrease Rnd every other rnd 6 times–48 sts remain (12-12-12-12).

FOOT

Work even until Foot measures 8", or 1½" less than desired length from back of Heel.

TOE

Decrease Rnd: *Needle 1:* Knit to last 3 sts, skp, k1; *Needle 2:* K1, k2tog, knit to end; *Needle 3:* Knit to last 3 sts, skp, k1; *Needle 4:* K1, k2tog, knit to end–44 sts remain. Knit 1 rnd.

Repeat Decrease Rnd every other rnd 3 times, then every rnd 3 times–20 sts remain (5-5-5-5). Knit to end of Needle 1.

FINISHING

Break yarn, leaving long tail. Transfer sts from Needle 1 to Needle 4, and sts from Needle 3 to Needle 2. Using Kitchener st (see General Techniques, page 140), graft Toe sts. Weave in ends. Block lightly.

KEY

- ⊡ **Purl on RS, knit on WS.**
- ⊠ **K1-tbl on RS, p1-tbl on WS.**
- ◯ **Yo**
- ⊠ **K2tog**
- ⊠ **Skp**
- ⊼ **S2kp2**
- ⦀ **K3 on RS, p3 on WS.**
- ⓷ **3-st lift:** Wyib, *insert right-hand needle into st 3 rows below next st on left-hand needle, draw up a loop*, yo; repeat from * to * once; drop st from left-hand needle, allowing it to unravel back to lifted st (see page 15).

Note: *Work Chart in-the-rnd for Leg and back and forth in rows for Heel Flap. Even-numbered rows will be WS rows when working back and forth.*

PATTERN A

samurai

The stitch pattern in these socks is strong yet fluid, and the name Samurai seemed fitting—reflecting a warrior with elaborate armor and very quick movements.

The original samurai came from the guards of the imperial palace. Their protective yet highly decorative armor, carefully honed martial arts skills, superbly crafted weapons, and deft swordsmanship made them formidable warriors from the sixth to the nineteenth century in Japan.

The socks are not difficult and are appropriate for either men or women. The 4-stitch cable pattern that begins in the ribbing at the top of the sock is repeated in the stitch design for the body of the sock, but sometimes turns left and sometimes right, the knitter's version of the unexpected movements in martial arts. The stitch pattern also includes panels of seed stitch, which add to the texture and strong appearance of these socks.

FINISHED MEASUREMENTS
7½" Foot circumference
10" Foot length from back of Heel
9½" Leg length to base of Heel

YARN
Kolláge Yarns Luscious (63% cotton / 37% nylon elastic; 55 grams / 185 yards): 2 hanks #6726 Walnut

NEEDLES
One set of five double-pointed needles (dpn) size US 2 (2.75 mm)
Change needle size if necessary to obtain correct gauge.

NOTIONS
Stitch marker; cable needle (cn)

GAUGE
26 sts and 35 rnds = 4" (10 cm) in Stockinette stitch (St st)

ABBREVIATIONS
C4B: Slip 2 sts to cn, hold to back, k2, k2 from cn.
C4F: Slip 2 sts to cn, hold to front, k2, k2 from cn.

KEY

□ **Knit**

⊡ **Purl**

C4B: Slip 2 sts to cn, hold to back, k2, k2 from cn.

C4F: Slip 2 sts to cn, hold to front, k2, k2 from cn.

PATTERN A

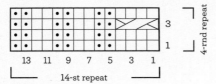

13 11 9 7 5 3 1

14-st repeat

4-rnd repeat

PATTERN B

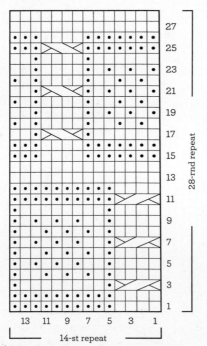

13 11 9 7 5 3 1

14-st repeat

28-rnd repeat

STITCH PATTERNS
PATTERN A
(multiple of 14 sts; 4-rnd repeat)

Rnds 1 and 2: *K4, [P2, k2] twice, p2; repeat from * to end.

Rnd 3: *C4B, [p2, k2] twice, p2; repeat from * to end.

Rnd 4: Repeat Rnd 1.

Repeat Rnds 1-4 for Pattern A.

PATTERN B
(multiple of 14 sts; 28-rnd repeat)

Rnds 1, 2, and 12: *K4, p10; repeat from * to end.

Rnd 3: *C4B, p1, k8, p1; repeat from * to end.

Rnds 4, 6, and 8: *K4, [p1, k1] 3 times, p1, k2, p1; repeat from * to end.

Rnds 5 and 9: *K4, p1, k2, [p1, k1] 3 times, p1; repeat from * to end.

Rnd 7: *C4B, p1, k2, [p1, k1] 3 times, p1; repeat from * to end.

Rnd 10: *K4, p1, k8, p1; repeat from * to end.

Rnd 11: *C4B, p10; repeat from * to end.

Rnds 13 and 14: Knit.

Rnds 15 and 16: *P7, k4, p3; repeat from * to end.

Rnd 17: *K6, p1, C4F, p1, k2; repeat from * to end.

Rnds 18, 20, and 22: *[K1, p1] twice, k2, p1, k4, p1, k1, p1; repeat from * to end.

Rnds 19 and 23: *[P1, k1] 3 times, p1, k4, p1, k2; repeat from * to end.

Rnd 21: *[P1, k1] 3 times, p1, C4F, p1, k2; repeat from * to end.

Rnd 24: *K6, p1, k4, p1, k2; repeat from * to end.

Rnd 25: *P7, C4F, p3; repeat from * to end.

Rnd 26: *P7, k4, p3; repeat from * to end.

Rnds 27 and 28: Knit.

Repeat Rnds 1-28 for Pattern B.

LEG

CO 56 sts. Divide sts evenly among 4 needles (14-14-14-14). Join for working in the rnd, being careful not to twist sts; place marker (pm) for beginning of rnd. Begin Pattern A; work even for 12 rnds.

Next Rnd: Change to Pattern B; work even until 2 vertical repeats of Pattern B have been completed, decrease 2 sts on each needle on last rnd–48 sts remain (12-12-12-12).

HEEL FLAP

Set-Up Row 1 (RS): K12, turn.
Set-Up Row 2: Slip 1, p23, working all 24 sts onto 1 needle for Heel Flap, and removing marker. Leave remaining 24 sts on 2 needles for instep.
Row 1: Working only on 24 Heel Flap sts, *slip 1, k1; repeat from * to end.
Row 2: Slip 1, purl to end.
Repeat Rows 1 and 2 eleven times.

TURN HEEL

Set-Up Row 1 (RS): Slip 1, k13, skp, k1, turn.
Set-Up Row 2: Slip 1, p5, p2tog, p1, turn.
Row 1: Slip 1, knit to 1 st before gap, skp (the 2 sts on either side of gap), k1, turn.
Row 2: Slip 1, purl to 1 st before gap, p2tog (the 2 sts on either side of gap), p1, turn.
Repeat Rows 1 and 2 three times, omitting final k1 and p1 sts in last repeat of Rows 1 and 2–14 sts remain.

GUSSET

Next Row (RS): *Needle 1:* Knit across Heel Flap sts, pick up and knit 13 sts along left side of Heel Flap, M1; *Needles 2 and 3:* Knit across sts on instep needles; *Needle 4:* M1, pick up and knit 13 sts along right side of Heel Flap, k7 from Needle 1. Join for working in the rnd; pm for beginning of rnd–66 sts (21-12-12-21).
Next Rnd: *Needle 1:* Knit to last 2 sts, skp; *Needles 2 and 3:* Knit; *Needle 4:* K2tog, knit to end–64 sts remain.
Decrease Rnd: *Needle 1:* Knit to last 3 sts, skp, k1; *Needles 2 and 3:* Knit; *Needle 4:* K1, k2tog, knit to end–62 sts remain (19-12-12-19). Work even for 1 rnd.
Repeat Decrease Rnd every other rnd 7 times–48 sts remain (12-12-12-12).

FOOT

Work even until Foot measures 8⅓", or 1⅛" less than desired length from back of Heel.

TOE

Decrease Rnd: *Needle 1:* Knit to last 3 sts, skp, k1; *Needle 2:* K1, k2tog, knit to end; *Needle 3:* Knit to last 3 sts, skp, k1; *Needle 4:* K1, k2tog, knit to end–44 sts remain. Knit 1 rnd.
Repeat Decrease Rnd every other rnd 3 times, then every rnd 3 times–20 sts remain (5-5-5-5). Knit to end of Needle 1.

FINISHING

Break yarn, leaving long tail. Transfer sts from Needle 1 to Needle 4, and sts from Needle 3 to Needle 2. Using Kitchener st (see General Techniques, page 140), graft Toe sts. Weave in ends. Block lightly.

kabuki

boot

Kabuki, a form of Japanese theater that originated in the early 1600s, is known for its style of drama, elaborate makeup, and special effects, such as revolving stages and trapdoors. Traditionally catering to the common people rather than the higher taste of the upper classes, kabuki remains popular today. The word *kabuki* derives from a word that means "out of the ordinary."

The flow of the design in these Kabuki Boot socks is something out of the ordinary, too. It features a small, decorative rib followed by a simple-to-work stitch pattern composed of cables and stitches twisted to the right or left. It's nothing fancy—yet the finished sock appears dramatic.

FINISHED MEASUREMENTS
8" Foot circumference
10" Foot length from back of Heel
7¾" Leg length to base of Heel

YARN
Brown Sheep Company Lamb's Pride Worsted (85% wool / 15% mohair; 4 ounces / 190 yards): 1 skein #M52 Spruce

NEEDLES
One set of five double-pointed needles (dpn) size US 5 (3.75 mm)
Change needle size if necessary to obtain correct gauge.

NOTIONS
Stitch marker; cable needle (cn)

GAUGE
20 sts and 30 rnds = 4" (10 cm) in Stockinette stitch (St st)

ABBREVIATIONS
RT: K2tog, but do not drop sts from left-hand needle, insert right-hand needle between 2 sts just worked and knit first st again, slip both sts from left-hand needle together.
LT: Knit into back of second st, then knit first and second sts together through back loops, slip both sts from left-hand needle together.
C3F: Slip next st to cn, hold to front, [k1-tbl] twice, k1-tbl from cn.
C6F: Slip 3 sts to cn, hold to front, k3, k3 from cn.

STITCH PATTERNS
PATTERN A
(multiple of 6 sts)

Rnds 1-4: *K1-tbl, p1; repeat from * to end.

Rnd 5: *LT, k1-tbl, RT, p1; repeat from * to end.

Rnd 6: *P1, [k1-tbl] 3 times, p2; repeat from * to end.

Rnd 7: *P1, C3F, p2; repeat from * to end.

PATTERN B
(multiple of 13 sts; 14-rnd repeat)

Rnds 1-4, 6, and 8-12: *P1, k5, p1, k6; repeat from * to end.

Rnd 5: *P1, yo, ssk, k1, k2tog, yo, p1, k6; repeat from * to end.

Rnd 7: *P1, k1, yo, s2kp2, yo, k1, p1, k6; repeat from * to end.

Rnd 13: *P1, k5, p1, C6F; repeat from * to end.

Rnd 14: Repeat Rnd 1.

Repeat Rnds 1-14 for Pattern B.

LEG
CO 48 sts. Divide sts evenly among 4 needles (12-12-12-12). Join for working in the rnd, being careful not to twist sts; place marker (pm) for beginning of rnd. Begin Pattern A; work even for 7 rnds. Knit 1 rnd, increase 1 st on each needle–52 sts (13-13-13-13).

Next Rnd: Change to Pattern B; work even until 2 vertical repeats of Pattern B have been completed. Knit 1 rnd, decrease 3 sts evenly across each needle–40 sts remain (10-10-10-10).

HEEL FLAP
Set-Up Row 1 (RS): K10, turn.

Set-Up Row 2: Slip 1, p19, working all 20 sts onto 1 needle for Heel Flap, and removing marker. Leave remaining 20 sts on 2 needles for instep.

Rnd 1: Working only on 20 Heel Flap sts, *slip 1, k1; repeat from * to end.

Rnd 2: Slip 1, purl to end.

Repeat Rnds 1 and 2 nine times.

TURN HEEL
Set-Up Row 1 (RS): Slip 1, k11, skp, k1, turn.

Set-Up Row 2: Slip 1, p5, p2tog, p1, turn.

Row 1: Slip 1, knit to 1 st before gap, skp (the 2 sts on either side of gap), k1, turn.

Row 2: Slip 1, purl to 1 st before gap, p2tog (the 2 sts on either side of gap), p1, turn.

Repeat Rows 1 and 2 twice, omitting final k1 and p1 in last Repeat of Rows 1 and 2–12 sts remain.

GUSSET

Next Row (RS): *Needle 1:* Knit across Heel Flap sts, pick up and knit 11 sts along left side of Heel Flap, M1; *Needles 2 and 3:* Knit across sts on instep needles; *Needle 4:* M1, pick up and knit 11 sts along right side of Heel Flap, k6 from Needle 1. Join for working in the rnd; pm for beginning of rnd–56 sts (18-10-10-18).
Next Rnd: Knit to last 2 sts, skp; *Needles 2 and 3:* Knit; *Needle 4:* K2tog, knit to end–54 sts remain.
Decrease Rnd: *Needle 1:* Knit to last 3 sts, skp, k1; *Needles 2 and 3:* Knit; *Needle 4:* K1, k2tog, knit to end–52 sts remain (16-10-10-16). Work even for 1 rnd.
Repeat Decrease Rnd every other rnd 6 times–40 sts remain (10-10-10-10).

FOOT

Work even until Foot measures 8½", or 1½" less than desired length from back of Heel.

TOE

Decrease Rnd: *Needle 1:* Knit to last 3 sts, skp, k1; *Needle 2:* K1, k2tog, knit to end; *Needle 3:* Knit to last 3 sts, skp, k1; *Needle 4:* K1, k2tog, knit to end–36 sts remain. Knit 1 rnd.
Repeat Decrease Rnd every other rnd 5 times–16 sts remain (4-4-4-4). Knit to end of Needle 1.

FINISHING

Break yarn, leaving long tail. Transfer sts from Needle 1 to Needle 4, and sts from Needle 3 to Needle 2. Using Kitchener st (see General Techniques, page 140), graft Toe sts. Weave in ends. Block lightly.

KEY

☐ Knit

⊡ Purl

Ⓡ K1-tbl

Ⓞ Yo

⊠ K2tog

⧄ Ssk

⩘ S2kp2

⬚ **RT:** K2tog, but do not drop sts from left-hand needle, insert right-hand needle between 2 sts just worked and knit first st again, slip both sts from left-hand needle together.

⬚ **LT:** Knit into back of second st, then knit first and second sts together through back loop, slip both sts from left-hand needle together.

⬚ **C3F:** Slip next st to cn, hold to front, [k1-tbl] twice, k1-tbl from cn.

⬚ **C6F:** Slip 3 sts to cn, hold to front, k3, k3 from cn.

PATTERN A

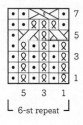

5   3   1

⌊ 6-st repeat ⌋

PATTERN B

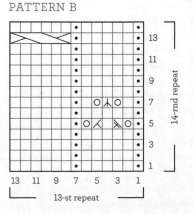

14-rnd repeat

13 11 9 7 5 3 1

⌊ 13-st repeat ⌋

tsunami

As we have seen in the last several years, tsunamis can be amazingly destructive events. A tsunami is actually a series of waves that is created when water is rapidly displaced by something like an earthquake, volcanic eruption, or underwater explosion. So why, you ask, would I name socks Tsunami?

When I saw this stitch pattern, I thought of the word *tsunami* right away, perhaps because of the peaceful little islands of purl stitches interrupted periodically by large cables, moving like waves. I discontinued the cable at the end of the sock top and let the small diamonds of purls move into the instep without the cable interruption. The sock is a bit longer than a regular crew sock, but not as long as a kneesock. I think of them as trouser socks, perfectly appropriate for either men or women.

FINISHED MEASUREMENTS
7½" Foot circumference
9½" Foot length from back of Heel
9½" Leg length to base of Heel

YARN
Regia Silk (55% wool / 25% polyamide / 20% silk; 50 grams / 220 yards): 2 skeins #091 Medium Gray

NEEDLES
One set of five double-pointed needles (dpn) size 1 (2.25 mm)
One set of five double-pointed needles size 2 (2.75 mm)
Change needle size if necessary to obtain correct gauge.

NOTIONS
Stitch marker; cable needle (cn)

GAUGE
30 sts and 42 rnds = 4" (10 cm) in Stockinette stitch (St st), using larger needles

ABBREVIATIONS
C8F: Slip 4 sts to cn, hold to front, k4, k4 from cn.

KEY

☐ Knit

⊡ Purl

⬚⬚⬚ C8F: Slip 4 sts to cn, hold to front, k4, k4 from cn.

PATTERN B

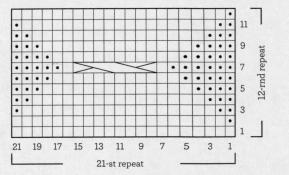

21-st repeat · 12-rnd repeat

PATTERN C

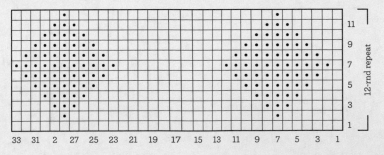

12-rnd repeat

78

STITCH PATTERNS

PATTERN A
(multiple of 4 sts; 1-rnd repeat)
All Rnds: *K2, p2; repeat from * to end.

PATTERN B
(multiple of 21 sts; 12-rnd repeat)
Rnd 1: Knit.
Rnd 2: *P1, k20; repeat from * to end.
Rnds 3 and 11: *P2, k18, p1; repeat from * to end.
Rnds 4 and 10: *P3, k16, p2; repeat from * to end.
Rnds 5 and 9: *P4, k14, p3; repeat from * to end.
Rnds 6 and 8: *P5, k12, p4; repeat from * to end.
Rnd 7: *P6, k1, C8F, k1, p5; repeat from * to end.
Rnd 12: Repeat Rnd 2.
Repeat Rnds 1-12 for Pattern B.

PATTERN C
(panel of 33 sts; 12-rnd repeat)
Rnd 1: Knit.
Rnd 2: K6, p1, k20, p1, k5.
Rnds 3 and 11: K5, p3, k18, p3, k4.
Rnds 4 and 10: K4, p5, k16, p5, k3.
Rnds 5 and 9: K3, p7, k14, p7, k2.
Rnds 6 and 8: K2, p9, k12, p9, k1.
Rnd 7: K1, p11, k10, p11.
Rnd 12: Repeat Rnd 2.
Repeat Rnds 1-12 for Pattern C.

LEG
Using smaller needles, CO 64 sts. Divide sts evenly among 4 needles (16-16-16-16). Join for working in the rnd, being careful not to twist sts; place marker (pm) for beginning of rnd. Begin Pattern A; work even for 13 rnds, decrease 1 st on last rnd–63 sts.

Next Rnd: Rearrange sts among 3 larger needles (21-21-21). Change to Pattern B; work even until 5 vertical repeats of Pattern B have been completed, then work Rnds 1-12, omitting cable on Rnd 7, and working cable sts in St st. Rearrange sts among 4 needles (15-17-16-15).

HEEL FLAP

Set-Up Row 1 (RS): K15, turn.
Set-Up Row 2: Slip 1, p29, working all 30 sts onto 1 needle for Heel Flap, and removing marker. Leave remaining 33 sts on 2 needles for instep.
Row 1: Working only on 30 Heel Flap sts, *slip 1, k1; repeat from * to end.
Row 2: Slip 1, purl to end.
Repeat Rows 1 and 2 eleven times.

TURN HEEL

Set-Up Row 1 (RS): Slip 1, k16, skp, k1, turn.
Set-Up Row 2: Slip 1, p5, p2tog, p1, turn.
Row 1: Slip 1, knit to 1 st before gap, skp (the 2 sts on either side of gap), k1, turn.
Row 2: Slip 1, purl to 1 st before gap, p2tog (the 2 sts on either side of gap), p1, turn.
Repeat Rows 1 and 2 four times–18 sts remain.

GUSSET

Next Rnd: *Needle 1:* Knit across Heel Flap sts, pick up and knit 13 sts along left side of Heel Flap, M1; *Needles 2 and 3:* Work Pattern C across instep sts; *Needle 4:* M1, pick up and knit 13 sts along right side of heel flap, k8 from Needle 1. Join for working in the rnd; pm for beginning of rnd–79 sts (23-17-16-23).

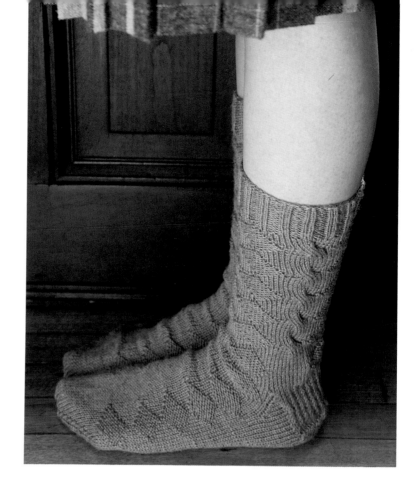

Next Rnd: *Needle 1:* Knit to last 2 sts, skp; *Needles 2 and 3:* Work even as established; *Needle 4:* K2tog, knit to end–77 sts remain.
Decrease Rnd: *Needle 1:* Knit to last 3 sts, skp, k1; *Needles 2 and 3:* Work even as established; *Needle 4:* K1, k2tog, knit to end–75 sts remain (21-17-16-21). Work even for 1 rnd. Repeat Decrease Rnd every other rnd 5 times–65 sts remain (16-17-16-16).

FOOT

Work even until Foot measures 8", or 1½" less than desired length from back of Heel.
Next Rnd: Change to St st (knit every rnd) across all sts, decrease 1 st on Needle 2–64 sts remain (16-16-16-16).

TOE

Decrease Rnd: *Needle 1:* Knit to last 3 sts, skp, k1; *Needle 2:* K1, k2tog, knit to end; *Needle 3:* Knit to last 3 sts, skp, k1; *Needle 4:* K1, k2tog, knit to end–60 sts remain. Knit 1 rnd.
Repeat Decrease Rnd every other rnd 10 times–20 sts remain (5-5-5-5). Knit to end of Needle 1.

FINISHING

Break yarn, leaving long tail. Transfer sts from Needle 1 to Needle 4, and sts from Needle 3 to Needle 2. Using Kitchener st (see General Techniques, page 140), graft Toe sts. Weave in ends. Block lightly.

karatsu

Karatsu is a style of Japanese pottery that originated sometime in the fifteenth or sixteenth century, and is noted for its glazes, which can range from earthy tones to deep blues. Sometimes painted with landscapes, pine trees, or bamboo, *Karatsu* takes the form of pots, vessels, and tea ware. Joanna Becker, author of *Karatsu Ware*, describes this simple, elegant pottery by saying, "Too much skill is evident on Karatsu ware to call it rustic; too much freedom and spontaneity to call it sophisticated. Its style lies somewhere between these two poles."

This very ornamental pattern requires some skill—it incorporates wrapped stitches and bobbles—but it also has a spontaneous, free-flowing feel. Like the pottery they're named for, these socks appear sophisticated without being too fussy.

FINISHED MEASUREMENTS
8½" Foot circumference
10¾" Foot length from back of Heel
13¾" Leg length to base of Heel

YARN
ShibuiKnits Sock (100% superwash merino wool; 50 grams / 191 yards):
3 hanks #S1601 Dragonfly

NEEDLES
One set of five double-pointed needles (dpn) size US 1 (2.25 mm)
Change needle size if necessary to obtain correct gauge.

NOTIONS
Stitch marker; cable needle (cn)

GAUGE
31 sts and 46 rnds = 4" (10 cm) in Stockinette stitch (St st)

ABBREVIATIONS
MB (Make Bobble): Knit into front, back, front, back, then front of next st to increase to 5 sts, pass second, third, fourth, then fifth st over first st and off needle.
Wrap5: Slip next 5 sts to cn, wrap yarn counterclockwise around base of sts twice; working across wrapped sts, [k1-tbl] twice, p1, [k1-tbl] twice from cn (see page 13).

STITCH PATTERNS

Pattern A
(multiple of 4 sts; 1-rnd repeat)
All Rnds: *K2, p2; repeat from * to end.

Pattern B
(multiple of 16 sts; 24-rnd repeat)
Rnd 1: *Yo, ssk, p3, wrap5, p3, k2tog, yo, p1; repeat from * to end.
Rnd 2: *K2, p3, [k1-tbl] twice, p1, [k1-tbl] twice, p3, k2, p1; repeat from * to end.
Rnd 3: *K2tog, yo, p2, k2tog, yo, k1-tbl, p1, k1-tbl, yo, skp, p2, yo, ssk, p1; repeat from * to end.
Rnd 4: *K2, p2, [k1-tbl, p1] 3 times, k1-tbl, p2, k2, p1; repeat from * to end.
Rnd 5: *Yo, ssk, p1, k2tog, p1, k1-tbl, yo, p1, yo, k1-tbl, p1, skp, p1, k2tog, yo, p1; repeat from * to end.
Rnd 6: *K2, [p1, k1-tbl] twice, k1, p1, k1, [k1-tbl, p1] twice, k2, p1; repeat from * to end.
Rnd 7: *K2tog, yo, k2tog, p1, k1-tbl, yo, k1, p1, k1, yo, k1-tbl, p1, skp, yo, ssk, p1; repeat from * to end.
Rnd 8: *K2, k1-tbl, p1, k1-tbl, k2, p1, k2, k1-tbl, p1, k1-tbl, k2, p1; repeat from * to end.
Rnd 9: *K1, k2tog, p1, k1-tbl, yo, k2, p1, k2, yo, k1-tbl, p1, skp, k1, p1; repeat from * to end.
Rnd 10: *K1, k1-tbl, p1, k1-tbl, k3, p1, k3, k1-tbl, p1, k1-tbl, k1, p1; repeat from * to end.
Rnd 11: *K2tog, p1, k1-tbl, yo, k2tog, k1, yo, p1, yo, k1, ssk, yo, k1-tbl, p1, skp, p1; repeat from * to end.
Rnd 12: *K1-tbl, p1, k1-tbl, k3, p3, k3, [k1-tbl, p1] twice; repeat from * to end.
Rnd 13: *Yo, sk2p, yo, k2tog, k1, yo, p3, yo, k1, ssk, yo, k3tog, yo, p1; repeat from * to end.
Rnd 14: *K1, k1-tbl, k4, p3, k4, k1-tbl, k1, p1; repeat from * to end.
Rnd 15: *K2tog, yo, k2tog, k1, yo, k1-tbl, p1, MB, p1, k1-tbl, yo, k1, ssk, yo, ssk, p1; repeat from * to end.
Rnd 16: *K4, p1, k1-tbl, p3, k1-tbl, p1, k4, p1; repeat from * to end.
Rnd 17: *Yo, ssk, k2tog, yo, p1, k1-tbl, p3, k1-tbl, p1, yo, ssk, k2tog, yo, p1; repeat from * to end.
Rnd 18: *K2, p1, k1, p1, k1-tbl, p3, k1-tbl, p1, k1, p1, k2, p1; repeat from * to end.
Rnd 19: *K2tog, yo, [p1, k1-tbl] twice, p3, [k1-tbl, p1] twice, yo, ssk, p1; repeat from * to end.
Rnd 20: *K2, [p1, k1-tbl] twice, p3, [k1-tbl, p1] twice, k2, p1; repeat from * to end.
Rnd 21: *Yo, ssk, p1, yo, k1-tbl, p1, skp, p1, k2tog, p1, k1-tbl, yo, p1, k2tog, yo, p1; repeat from * to end.
Rnd 22: *K2, p2, [k1-tbl, p1] 3 times, k1-tbl, p2, k2, p1; repeat from * to end.
Rnd 23: *K2tog, yo, p2, yo, skp, k1-tbl, p1, k1-tbl, k2tog, yo, p2, yo, ssk, p1; repeat from * to end.
Rnd 24: Repeat Rnd 2.
Repeat Rnds 1-24 for Pattern B.

Pattern C
(panel of 5 sts; 4-rnd repeat)
Rnd 1: K2tog, yo, p1, yo, ssk.
Rnd 2: K2, p1, k2.
Rnd 3: Yo, ssk, p1, k2tog, yo.
Rnd 4: Repeat Rnd 2.
Repeat Rnds 1-4 for Pattern C.

LEG
CO 96 sts. Divide sts evenly among 4 needles (24-24-24-24). Join for working in the rnd, being careful not to twist sts; place marker (pm) for beginning of rnd. Begin Pattern A; work even for 15 rnds.
Next Rnd: Redistribute sts (32-16-16-32). Work in Pattern A as established over 16 sts, work in Pattern B over 64 sts, work in Pattern A as established to end. Work even for 4 rnds.

Shape Calf: Continuing in pattern as established, decrease 2 sts this rnd, then every 6 rnds 15 times, as follows: Work 2 sts together, work to last 2 sts, work 2 sts together–64 sts remain (16-16-16-16). *Note: To maintain rib pattern while decreasing, if second st of rnd is a knit st, work k2tog; if second st is a purl st, work p2tog. If next-to-last st of rnd is a knit st, work skp; if next-to-last st is a purl st, work p2tog. Work even until 4 vertical repeats of Pattern B have been completed, then work Rnds 1-16 once.*

HEEL FLAP
Set-Up Row 1 (RS): K16, turn.
Set-Up Row 2: Slip 1, k31, working all 32 sts onto 1 needle for Heel Flap, and removing marker. Leave remaining 32 sts on 2 needles for instep.
Row 1: Working only on 32 Heel Flap sts, *slip 1, k1; repeat from * to end.
Row 2: Slip 1, purl to end.
Repeat Rows 1 and 2 eleven times.

TURN HEEL
Set-Up Row 1 (RS): Slip 1, k17, skp, k1, turn.
Set-Up Row 2: Slip 1, p5, p2tog, p1, turn.
Row 1: Slip 1, knit to 1 st before gap, skp (the 2 sts on either side of gap), k1, turn.
Row 2: Slip 1, purl to 1 st before gap, p2tog (the 2 sts on either side of gap), p1, turn.
Repeat Rows 1 and 2 five times, omitting final k1 and p1 sts in last repeat of Rows 1 and 2–18 sts remain.

GUSSET
Next Row (RS): *Needle 1:* Knit across Heel Flap sts, pick up and knit 13 sts along left side of Heel Flap, M1; *Needle 2:* K14, work in

KEY

- ☐ Knit
- ⊡ Purl
- ⚇ K1-tbl
- ⊙ Yo
- ⊠ K2tog
- ⊠ Skp
- ⊠ Ssk
- ⊠ Sk2p
- ⊠ K3tog
- ⦿ **MB:** Knit into front, back, front, back then front of next st to increase to 5 sts; pass second, third, fourth, then fifth st, 1 at a time, over first st and off needle.
- ⟨⚇⚇·⚇⚇⟩ **Wrap5:** Slip next 5 sts to cn, wrap yarn counterclockwise around base of sts twice; working across wrapped sts, [k1-tbl] twice, p1, [k1-tbl] twice from cn (see page 13).

PATTERN B

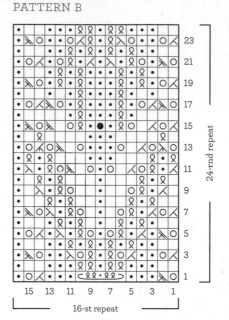

24-rnd repeat (rows 1–23, odd numbered)

16-st repeat (sts 15, 13, 11, 9, 7, 5, 3, 1)

PATTERN C

(rows 1, 3)

5-st repeat (sts 5, 3, 1)

Pattern C over next 5 sts, working 3 sts from Needle 3 onto Needle 2; *Needle 3:* K13; *Needle 4:* M1, pick up and knit 13 sts along right side of Heel Flap, k9 from Needle 1. Join for working in the rnd; pm for beginning of rnd–78 sts (23-19-13-23).

Next Rnd: *Needle 1:* Knit to last 2 sts, skp; *Needles 2 and 3:* Work even as established; *Needle 4:* K2tog, knit to end–76 sts remain.

Decrease Rnd: *Needle 1:* Knit to last 3 sts, skp, k1; *Needles 2 and 3:* Work even as established; *Needle 4:* K1, k2tog, knit to end–74 sts remain (21-19-13-21). Work even for 1 rnd. Repeat Decrease Rnd every other rnd 5 times–64 sts remain (16-19-13-16).

FOOT

Work even until Foot measures 9¼", or 1½" less than desired length from back of Heel. Redistribute sts (16-16-16-16).

Next Rnd: Change to St st (knit every rnd) across all sts. *Note: If you prefer, you may continue to work Instep pattern on Needle 2 until rnd before final Toe Decrease Rnd.*

TOE

Decrease Rnd: *Needle 1:* Knit to last 3 sts, skp, k1; *Needle 2:* K1, k2tog, knit to end; *Needle 3:* Knit to last 3 sts, skp, k1; *Needle 4:* K1, k2tog, knit to end–60 sts remain. Knit 2 rnds. Repeat Decrease Rnd every 3 rnds twice, then every rnd 10 times–20 sts remain (5-5-5-5). Knit to end of Needle 1.

FINISHING

Break yarn, leaving long tail. Transfer sts from Needle 1 to Needle 4, and sts from Needle 3 to Needle 2. Using Kitchener st (see General Techniques, page 140), graft Toe sts. Weave in ends. Block lightly.

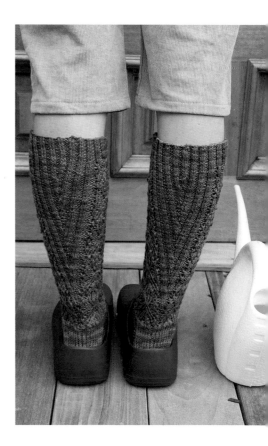

Knitted Socks East and West

hanami

lace

The Japanese custom of *hanami*—enjoying flowers—is centuries old. Originally, *hanami* included many kinds of blossoms, but it has since become analogous to viewing the cherry blossoms, also called *sakura*. To this day, thousands of people gather in Japanese parks each spring to hold feasts under the flowering cherry trees.

These socks are made of lace-weight yarn and feature a lace pattern that appears to be petals or leaves joined by pkoks. Weaving the pattern together is a fine lace design that appears to bend to and fro. These delicate socks aren't designed to wear with your everyday shoes, but rather with your nightgown as you relax on your chaise lounge with a beautiful vase of flowers nearby. If desired, you can continue the lace pattern into the foot; here, I chose to keep the fabric of the foot as solid as possible given the delicate quality of the yarn.

FINISHED MEASUREMENTS
8" Foot circumference
8¼" Foot length from back of Heel
6½" Leg length to base of Heel

YARN
Alpaca with a Twist Fino (70% baby alpaca / 30% silk; 100 grams / 875 yards): 1 hank #0098 Silver Belle

NEEDLES
One set of five double-pointed needles (dpn) size US 3 (3.25 mm)
Change needle size if necessary to obtain correct gauge.

NOTIONS
Stitch marker

GAUGE
24 sts and 37 rnds = 4" (10 cm) in Stockinette stitch (St st)

ABBREVIATIONS
Pkok: Slip third st on left-hand needle over first 2 sts and off needle; k1, yo, k1 (see page 12).

KEY

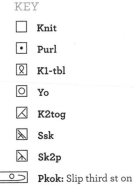

- ☐ Knit
- ⊡ Purl
- ⊠ K1-tbl
- ⊡ Yo
- ◻ K2tog
- ◻ Ssk
- ◻ Sk2p
- ⬜ Pkok: Slip third st on left-hand needle over first 2 sts and off needle; k1, yo, k1 (see page 12).

PATTERN B

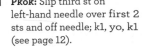

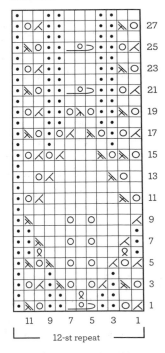

11 9 7 5 3 1

⌞ 12-st repeat ⌟

PATTERN A
(multiple of 2 sts; 1-rnd repeat)
Rnd 1: *K1, p1; repeat from * to end.
Rnd 2: Purl the knit sts and knit the purl sts as they face you.
Repeat Rnd 2 for Pattern A.

PATTERN B
(multiple of 12 sts)
Rnd 1: *K2tog, yo, p2, pkok, p2, yo, ssk, p1; repeat from * to end.
Rnd 2: *K2, p2, k1, k1-tbl, k1, p2, k2, p1; repeat from * to end.
Rnd 3: *Yo, ssk, p1, k2tog, yo, k1, yo, ssk, p1, k2tog, yo, p1; repeat from * to end.
Rnd 4: *K2, p1, k5, p1, k2, p1; repeat from * to end.
Rnd 5: *K2tog, yo, k2tog, [k1, yo] twice, k1, ssk, yo, ssk, p1; repeat from * to end.
Rnd 6: *P1, k1-tbl, k7, k1-tbl, p2; repeat from * to end.
Rnd 7: *P1, k2tog, k2, yo, k1, yo, k2, ssk, p2; repeat from * to end.
Rnd 8: *P1, k9, p2; repeat from * to end.
Rnd 9: *K2tog, k3, yo, k1, yo, k3, ssk, p1; repeat from * to end.
Rnds 10, 12, and 14: *K11, p1; repeat from * to end.
Rnd 11: *Yo, ssk, k7, k2tog, yo, p1; repeat from * to end.
Rnd 13: *K1, yo, ssk, k5, k2tog, yo, k1, p1; repeat from * to end.
Rnd 15: *[Yo, ssk] twice, k3, [k2tog, yo] twice, p1; repeat from * to end.
Rnds 16: *K2, p1, k5, p1, k2, p1; repeat from * to end.
Rnd 17: *K2tog, yo, p1, yo, ssk, k1, k2tog, yo, p1, yo, ssk, p1; repeat from * to end.
Rnds 18, 20, 22, 24, and 26: *K2, p2, k3, p2, k2, p1; repeat from * to end.
Rnd 19: *Yo, ssk, p2, yo, sk2p, yo, p2, k2tog, yo, p1; repeat from * to end.

Rnds 21 and 25: *K2tog, yo, p2, pkok, p2, yo, ssk, p1; repeat from * to end.

Rnds 23 and 27: *Yo, ssk, p2, k3, p2, k2tog, yo, p1; repeat from * to end.

Rnd 28: Repeat Rnd 26.

LEG

CO 48 sts. Divide sts evenly among 4 needles (12-12-12-12). Join for working in the rnd, being careful not to twist sts; place marker (pm) for beginning of rnd. Begin Pattern A; work even for 8 rnds.

Next Rnd: Change to Pattern B; work rnds 1-28 once, then rnds 1-20 once.

HEEL FLAP

Set-Up Row 1 (RS): K12, turn.

Set-Up Row 2: Slip 1, p23, working all 24 sts onto 1 needle for Heel Flap, and removing marker. Leave remaining 24 sts on 2 needles for instep.

Row 1: Working only on 24 Heel Flap sts, *slip 1, k1; repeat from * to end.

Row 2: Slip 1, purl to end. Repeat Rows 1 and 2 eleven times.

TURN HEEL

Set-Up Row 1 (RS): Slip 1, k13, skp, k1, turn.

Set-Up Row 2: Slip 1, p5, p2tog, p1, turn.

Row 1: Slip 1, knit to 1 st before gap, skp (the 2 sts on either side of gap), k1, turn.

Row 2: Slip 1, purl to 1 st before gap, p2tog (the 2 sts on either side of gap), p1, turn. Repeat Rows 1 and 2 three times, omitting final k1 and p1 sts in last repeat of Rows 1 and 2–14 sts remain.

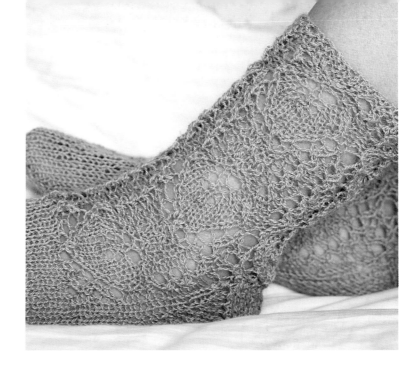

GUSSET

Next Row (RS): *Needle 1:* Knit across Heel Flap sts, pick up and knit 13 sts along left side of Heel Flap, M1; *Needles 2 and 3:* Continue Pattern B as established; *Needle 4:* M1, pick up and knit 13 sts along right side of Heel Flap, k7 from Needle 1. Join for working in the rnd; pm for beginning of rnd–66 sts (21-12-12-21).

Next Rnd: *Needle 1:* Knit to last 2 sts, skp; *Needles 2 and 3:* Work even as established; *Needle 4:* K2tog, knit to end–64 sts remain.

Decrease Rnd: *Needle 1:* Knit to last 3 sts, skp, k1; *Needles 2 and 3:* Work even as established; *Needle 4:* K1, k2tog, knit to end–62 sts remain (19-12-12-19). Work even for 1 rnd. Repeat Decrease Rnd every other rnd 7 times–48 sts remain (12-12-12-12).

FOOT

Work even until Rnd 19 of Pattern B is complete. Change to St st (knit every rnd) across all sts; work even until Foot measures 6¾", or 1½" less than desired length from back of Heel.

TOE

Decrease Rnd: *Needle 1:* Knit to last 3 sts, skp, k1; *Needle 2:* K1, k2tog, knit to end; *Needle 3:* Knit to last 3 sts, skp, k1; *Needle 4:* K1, k2tog, knit to end–44 sts remain. Knit 1 rnd.

Repeat Decrease Rnd every other rnd 3 times, then every rnd 4 times–16 sts remain (4-4-4-4).

FINISHING

Break yarn, leaving long tail. Transfer sts from Needle 1 to Needle 4, and sts from Needle 3 to Needle 2. Using Kitchener st (see General Techniques, page 140), graft Toe sts. Weave in ends. Block lightly.

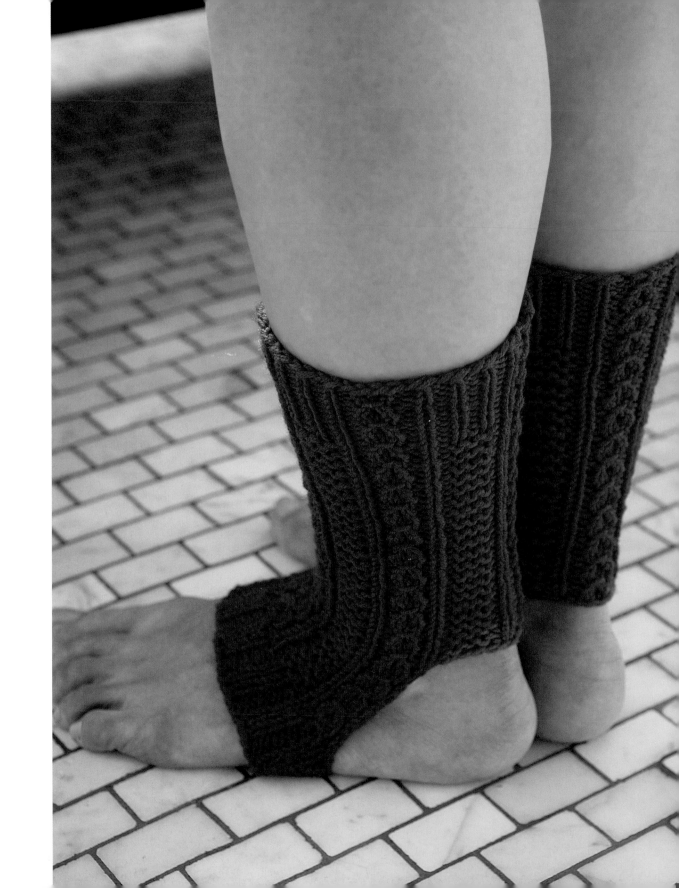

obi

yoga

The obi is a sash worn with various styles of Japanese clothing to secure it in place and to enhance the shape of the body. Obi are worn with kimonos by both men and women and are traditionally made of silk, often in colorful, decorative designs.

The Obi Yoga socks feature a pattern that integrates the ribbing and the body and uses the pkok maneuver, alternated with garter stitch, to create obilike bands in the design. These unusual socks have no heel or toe, but rather a stirrup that slides under the instep of the foot. This construction makes them particularly useful during yoga classes, where the exposed foot allows for better traction on the floor or mat. They're also perfect when you are getting a pedicure or when you simply want to wear socks with flip-flops for any reason.

FINISHED MEASUREMENTS
7" Leg circumference
6½" Leg length to Heel Opening

YARN
Debbie Bliss Baby Cashmerino
(55% merino wool / 33% microfiber / 12% cashmere; 50 grams / 137 yards):
2 skeins #023 Sienna

NEEDLES
One set of five double-pointed needles (dpn) size US 2 (2.75 mm)
Change needle size if necessary to obtain correct gauge.

NOTIONS
Stitch marker

GAUGE
28 sts and 34 rnds = 4" (10 cm) in Stockinette stitch (St st)

ABBREVIATIONS
Pkok: Slip third st on left-hand needle over first 2 sts and off needle; k1, yo, k1 (see page 12).

KEY

☐ **Knit on RS, purl on WS.**

⊡ **Purl on RS, knit on WS.**

⊏o⊐ **Pkok:** Slip third st on left-hand needle over first 2 sts and off needle; k1, yo, k1 (see page 12).

PATTERN A

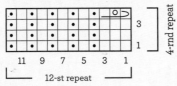

11 9 7 5 3 1

12-st repeat

4-rnd repeat

PATTERN B

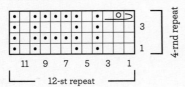

11 9 7 5 3 1

12-st repeat

4-rnd repeat

PATTERN C

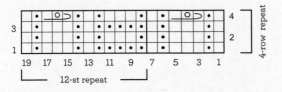

19 17 15 13 11 9 7 5 3 1

12-st repeat

4-row repeat

STITCH PATTERNS

PATTERN A
(multiple of 12 sts; 4-rnd repeat)

Rnds 1-3: *K3, [p1, k1] 4 times, p1; repeat from * to end.

Rnd 4: *Pkok, [p1, k1] 4 times, p1; repeat from * to end.

Repeat Rnds 1-4 for Pattern A.

PATTERN B
(multiple of 12 sts; 4-rnd repeat)

Rnds 1 and 3: *K3, p1, k1, p1, k3, p1, k1, p1; repeat from * to end.

Rnd 2: *K3, p1, k1, p5, k1, p1; repeat from * to end.

Rnd 4: *Pkok, p1, k1, p5, k1, p1; repeat from * to end.

Repeat Rnds 1-4 for Pattern B.

PATTERN C
(multiple of 12 sts + 7; 4-row repeat)

Rows 1 and 3 (WS): [P1, k1, p3, k1, p1, k5] twice, p1, k1, p3, k1, p1.

Row 2: K1, p1, k3, p1, k1, [p1, k3, p1, k1, p1, k3, p1, k1] twice.

Row 4: K1, p1, pkok, p1, k1, [p1, k3, p1, k1, p1, pkok, p1, k1] twice.

Repeat Rows 1-4 for Pattern C.

PATTERN D
(multiple of 4 sts; 1-rnd repeat)

All Rnds: *K2, p2; repeat from * to end.

LEG

CO 48 sts. Divide sts evenly among 4 needles (12-12-12-12). Join for working in the rnd, being careful not to twist sts; place marker (pm) for beginning of rnd. Begin Pattern A; work even for 12 rnds.

Next Rnd: Change to Pattern B; work even until 10 vertical repeats of Pattern B have been completed, then work Rnds 1 and 2 once.

Heel Opening (RS): *Needles 1-3:* Work even; *Needle 4:* Work 5 sts, BO next 17 sts knitwise (7 sts on Needle 4 and 10 sts on Needle 1), work to BO sts–31 sts remain.

INSTEP

Next Row (WS): Change to Pattern C. Working all 31 sts onto 1 needle, and working back and forth, work even until instep measures 1½" from beginning of Heel Opening, ending with a RS row; do not turn.

STIRRUP

Next Row (WS): Transfer sts to 2 needles. Using third needle and Cable CO (see General Techniques, page 140), CO 17 sts; do not turn–48 sts. Redistribute sts among 4 needles (12-12-12-12).

Next Rnd (RS): Join for working in the rnd; pm for beginning of rnd. Change to Pattern D; work even until Stirrup measures 1". BO all sts in pattern.
Weave in ends. Block lightly.

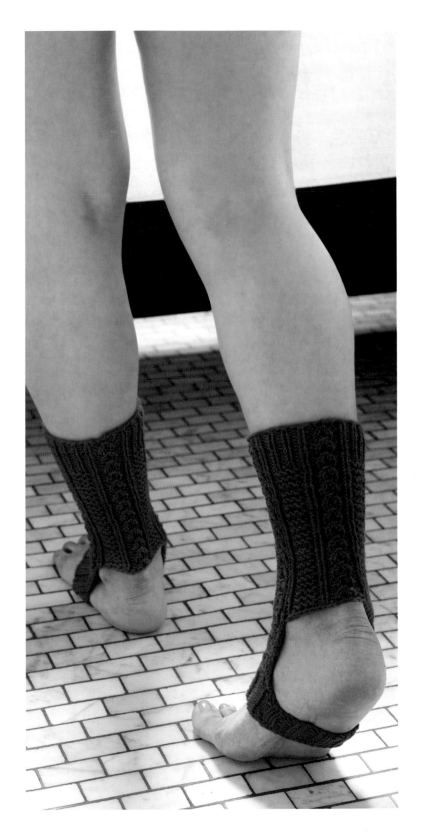

inro

hiking

The Japanese *inro* is a small, ornate case consisting of a stack of small, nested boxes. Because traditional Japanese clothing had no pockets, objects were held in *inro*, which were hung from the sash worn on the kimono. Once considered useful and necessary, they are now more admired for their art and craftsmanship.

The Inro Hiking socks have a series of decorative designs that are separated by wrapped stitches, reminiscent of the "stacks" of the Japanese *inro*. The wrap stitch, often seen in Japanese patterns, is very easy to work. These socks provide a nice, thick lining in hiking boots.

FINISHED MEASUREMENTS
8½" Foot circumference
10" Foot length from back of Heel
10¾" Leg length to base of Heel

YARN
Imperial Stock Ranch 2-Ply Wool
(100% wool; 4 ounces / 200 yards):
2 hanks #02 Pearl Gray

NEEDLES
One set of five double-pointed needles
(dpn) size US 5 (3.75 mm)
Change needle size if necessary to
obtain correct gauge.

NOTIONS
Stitch marker; cable needle (cn)

GAUGE
19 sts and 27 rnds = 4" (10 cm) in
Stockinette stitch (St st)

ABBREVIATIONS
Wrap6: Slip next 6 sts to cn, wrap yarn counterclockwise around base of sts twice, knit the 6 wrapped sts (see page 13).
Wrap4: Slip next 4 sts to cn, wrap yarn counterclockwise around base of sts twice, knit the 4 wrapped sts (see page 13).

STITCH PATTERNS

PATTERN A
(multiple of 2 sts; 1-rnd repeat)
All Rnds: *K1, p1; repeat from * to end.

PATTERN B
(multiple of 14 sts; 16-rnd repeat)
Rnd 1: *P2, k4, p2, wrap6; repeat from * to end.
Rnds 2, 4, 6, and 8: *P2, k4, [p2, k2] twice; repeat from * to end.
Rnd 3: *P2, wrap4, p2, k6; repeat from * to end.
Rnds 5 and 7: *P2, k4, p2, k6; repeat from * to end.
Rnds 9 and 10: *P2, k4, p8; repeat from * to end.
Rnd 11: *P2, wrap4, p8; repeat from * to end.
Rnds 12-16: Repeat Rnd 9.
Repeat Rnds 1-16 for Pattern B.

LEG
CO 42 sts. Divide sts evenly among 3 needles (14-14-14). Join for working in the rnd, being careful not to twist sts; place marker (pm) for beginning of rnd. Begin Pattern A; work even for 11 rnds.
Next Rnd: Change to Pattern B; work even until 3 vertical repeats of Pattern B have been completed, decrease 2 sts evenly spaced on last rnd–40 sts remain. Redistribute sts evenly among 4 needles (10-10-10-10).

HEEL FLAP
Set-Up Row 1 (RS): K10, turn.
Set-Up Row 2: Slip 1, p19, working all 20 sts onto 1 needle for Heel Flap, and removing marker. Leave remaining 20 sts on 2 needles for instep.
Row 1: Working only on 20 Heel Flap sts, *slip 1, k1; repeat from * to end.
Row 2: Slip 1, purl to end.
Repeat Rows 1 and 2 nine times.

TURN HEEL
Set-Up Row 1 (RS): Slip 1, k11, skp, k1, turn.
Set-Up Row 2: Slip 1, p5, p2tog, p1, turn.
Row 2: Slip 1, knit to 1 st before gap, skp (the 2 sts on either side of gap), k1, turn.
Row 2: Slip 1, purl to 1 st before gap, p2tog (the 2 sts on either side of gap), p1, turn.
Repeat Rows 1 and 2 twice, omitting final k1 and p1 sts in last repeat of Rows 1 and 2–12 sts remain.

GUSSET

Next Row (RS): *Needle 1:* Knit across Heel Flap sts, pick up and knit 11 sts along left side of Heel Flap, M1; *Needles 2 and 3:* Knit across sts on instep needles; *Needle 4:* M1, pick up and knit 11 sts along right side of Heel Flap, k6 from Needle 1. Join for working in the rnd; pm for beginning of rnd–56 sts (18-10-10-18).

Next Rnd: *Needle 1:* Knit to last 2 sts, skp; *Needles 2 and 3:* Knit; *Needle 4:* K2tog, knit to end–54 sts remain.

Decrease Rnd: *Needle 1:* Knit to last 3 sts, skp, k1; *Needles 2 and 3:* Knit; *Needle 4:* K1, k2tog, knit to end–52 sts remain (16-10-10-16). Work even for 1 rnd.

Repeat Decrease Rnd every other rnd 6 times–40 sts remain (10-10-10-10).

FOOT

Work even until Foot measures 8½", or 1½" less than desired length from back of Heel.

TOE

Decrease Rnd: *Needle 1:* Knit to last 3 sts, skp, k1; *Needle 2:* K1, k2tog, knit to end; *Needle 3:* Knit to last 3 sts, skp, k1; *Needle 4:* K1, k2tog, knit to end–36 sts remain. Knit 1 rnd.

Repeat Decrease Rnd every other rnd 5 times–16 sts remain (4-4-4-4). Knit to end of Needle 1.

FINISHING

Break yarn, leaving long tail. Transfer sts from Needle 1 to Needle 4, and sts from Needle 3 to Needle 2. Using Kitchener st (see General Techniques, page 140), graft Toe sts. Weave in ends. Block lightly.

KEY

☐ **Knit**

⊡ **Purl**

Wrap6: Slip next 6 sts to cn, wrap yarn counterclockwise around base of sts twice, knit the 6 wrapped sts (see page 13).

Wrap4: Slip next 4 sts to cn, wrap yarn counterclockwise around base of sts twice, knit the 4 wrapped sts (see page 13).

PATTERN B

∞ **95**

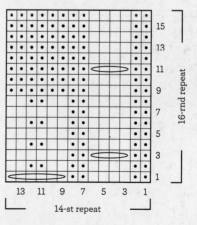

13   11   9   7   5   3   1

14-st repeat

16-rnd repeat

15
13
11
9
7
5
3
1

kyoto
cable

The Japanese city Kyoto was drawn into the spotlight after it hosted the 1997 conference that produced the Kyoto Protocol, which sought to decrease global greenhouse gas emissions. But long before that, Kyoto had a rich history of its own, which included it becoming the seat of the Japanese imperial court in 794. The word *Kyoto* is believed to come from the words "tranquility and peace capital."

I believe the pattern of Kyoto Cable also conveys peace and tranquility with its simple, rhythmic flow. The design includes one of the rather unique features I noticed in many Japanese patterns—a bit of lace surrounded by rows of garter stitch. This pattern is relatively simple and "peaceful" to knit, as well, including only simple stitches and an occasional cable crossing.

FINISHED MEASUREMENTS
12" circumference at widest point, slightly stretched
9" circumference at narrowest point, slightly stretched
23" long

YARN
Lorna's Laces Shepherd Worsted Yarn (100% superwash wool; 4 ounces / 225 yards): 2 hanks #14ns Denim
Note: If you wish to make these Leg Warmers longer than the given length, you will need 1 additional hank.

NEEDLES
One 16" (40 cm) circular (circ) needle size US 5 (3.75 mm)
One set of five double-pointed needles (dpn) size US 5 (3.75 mm)
One set of five double-pointed needles size US 4 (3.5 mm)
Change needle size if necessary to obtain correct gauge.

NOTIONS
Stitch markers; cable needle (cn)

GAUGE
20 sts and 24 rnds = 4" (10 cm) in Stockinette stitch (St st) using smaller needles

ABBREVIATIONS
C5F: Slip 2 sts to cn, hold to front, k3, k2 from cn.

STITCH PATTERNS

PATTERN A

(multiple of 7 sts; 24-rnd repeat)

Rnds 1, 3, 7, and 9-16: *K5, p2; repeat from * to end.

Rnds 2, 4, 6, and 8: Purl.

Rnd 5: *K1, [yo, skp] twice, p2; repeat from * to end.

Rnds 17: *C5F, p2; repeat from * to end.

Rnds 18-24: Repeat Rnd 1.
Repeat Rnds 1-24 for Pattern A.

LEG

Note: Change to larger dpn when necessary for number of sts on needle. Using circ needle, CO 73 sts. Join for working in the rnd, being careful not to twist sts; place marker (pm) for beginning of rnd.

Begin Pattern: [K2, p2] 3 times, pm, work in Pattern A over 49 sts, pm, [k2, p2] 3 times. Work even for 11 rnds.

Shape Calf: *Note: The decreases on the two leg warmers in the photo at left were each worked slightly differently. By following these instructions, you will create a leg warmer that looks like the one on the left side in the photo.* Decrease 2 sts this rnd, then every 12 rnds 11 times, as follows: Work 2 sts together, work to last 2 sts, work 2 sts together—49 sts remain. *Note: To maintain rib pattern while decreasing, if second st of rnd is a knit st, work k2tog; if second st is a purl st, work p2tog. If next-to-last st of rnd is a knit st, work skp; if next-to-last st is a purl st, work p2tog.* AT THE SAME TIME, when piece measures 8" from the beginning, change to smaller dpn. Work even until 6 vertical repeats of Pattern A have been completed, then work Rnds 1-8 once. BO all sts loosely.
Weave in ends. Block lightly.

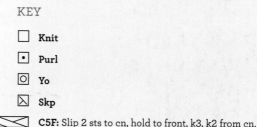

KEY

☐ **Knit**

⊡ **Purl**

⊡ **Yo**

⊠ **Skp**

⬲ **C5F:** Slip 2 sts to cn, hold to front, k3, k2 from cn.

PATTERN A

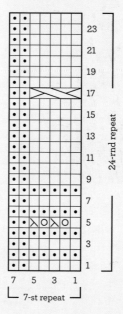

7-st repeat

24-rnd repeat

~ **99**

karate
cable

From a physical standpoint, karate is a series of punches, kicks, and knee and elbow strikes used in self-defense, but equally important is an emphasis on psychological elements such as persever-ance, fearlessness, virtue, and leadership skills. How can a small, lightweight woman take down a man twice her size with little apparent effort? The secret is in calling up physical, mental, and spiritual strength and focusing it into one small area. As such, karate can be seen as a form of meditation—centered and powerful at the same time.

The length and complexity of the cables in these socks bring the quick and unexpected movements of karate to mind, but knitting them also can be meditative—there are long stretches where little attention is required and the mind can focus on other things, then several rounds of intense concen-tration. The pattern isn't really difficult, using mostly simple knits, purls, and cable techniques.

FINISHED MEASUREMENTS
7½" Foot circumference
9½" Foot length from back of Heel
12" Leg length to base of Heel

YARN
S.R. Kertzer On Your Toes Bamboo
(75% bamboo / 25% nylon; 100 grams / 328 yards):
1 skein #ON260832 Sea Life Gray

NEEDLES
One set of five double-pointed needles
(dpn) size US 2 (2.75 mm)
One set of five double-pointed needles size
US 3 (3.25 mm)
Change needle size if necessary to obtain
correct gauge.

NOTIONS
Stitch marker; cable needle (cn)

GAUGE
25 sts and 34 rnds = 4" (10 cm) in Stockinette
stitch (St st), using smaller needles

ABBREVIATIONS
RT: K2tog, but do not drop sts from left-hand needle, insert right-hand needle between 2 sts just worked and knit first st again, slip both sts from left-hand needle together.
LT: Knit into back of second st, then knit first and second sts together through back loops, slip both sts from left-hand needle together.
C3F: Slip next st to cn, hold to front, [k1-tbl] twice, k1-tbl from cn.
C3B: Slip next st to cn, hold to back, [k1-tbl] twice, k1-tbl from cn.
C4B: Slip 2 sts to cn, hold to back, k2, k2 from cn.
C4F: Slip 2 sts to cn, hold to front, k2, k2 from cn.

Next Rnd: Change to larger needles and Pattern B; work even until 3 vertical repeats of Pattern B have been completed, decrease 1 st on each needle on last rnd–48 sts remain (12-12-12-12).

HEEL FLAP

Set-Up Row 1 (RS): Change to smaller needles. K12, turn.
Set-Up Row 2: Slip 1, p23, working all 24 sts onto 1 needle for Heel Flap, and removing marker. Leave remaining 24 sts on 2 needles for instep.
Row 1: Working only on 24 Heel Flap sts, *slip 1, k1; repeat from * to end.
Row 2: Slip 1, purl to end.
Repeat Rows 1 and 2 eleven times.

TURN HEEL

Set-Up Row 1 (RS): Slip 1, k13, skp, k1, turn.
Set-Up Row 2: Slip 1, p5, p2tog, p1, turn.
Row 1: Slip 1, knit to 1 st before gap, skp (the 2 sts on either side of gap), k1, turn.
Row 2: Slip 1, purl to 1 st before gap, p2tog (the 2 sts on either side of gap), p1, turn.
Repeat Rows 1 and 2 three times, omitting final k1 and p1 sts in last repeat of Rows 1 and 2–14 sts remain.

GUSSET

Next Row (RS): *Needle 1:* Knit across Heel Flap sts, pick up and knit 13 sts along left side of Heel Flap, M1; *Needles 2 and 3:* Knit across sts on instep needles; *Needle 4:* M1, pick up and knit 13 sts along right side of Heel Flap, k7 from Needle 1. Join for working in the rnd; pm for beginning of rnd–66 sts (21-12-12-21).

STITCH PATTERNS

PATTERN A
(multiple of 6 sts)

Rnds 1-5: *K1-tbl, p1; repeat from * to end.
Rnd 6: *LT, k1-tbl, RT, p1; repeat from * to end.
Rnds 7, 9, 11, 13, and 15: *P1, [k1-tbl] 3 times, p2; repeat from * to end.
Rnds 8 and 12: *P1, C3F, p2; repeat from * to end.
Rnds 10 and 14: *P1, C3B, p2; repeat from * to end.
Rnd 16: *RT, k1-tbl, LT, p1; repeat from * to end.
Rnd 17-21: Repeat Rnd 1.

PATTERN B
(multiple of 13 sts; 20-rnd repeat)

Rnds 1, 5, and 9: *K1-tbl, p2, k2, C4B, k2, p2; repeat from * to end.
Rnds 2, 4, 6, and 8: *K1-tbl, p2, k8, p2; repeat from * to end.
Rnds 3 and 7: *K1-tbl, p2, [C4F] twice, p2; repeat from * to end.
Rnds 10-20: Repeat Rnd 2.
Repeat Rnds 1-20 for Pattern B.

LEG

Using smaller needles, CO 48 sts. Divide sts evenly among 4 needles (12-12-12-12). Begin Pattern A; work even for 21 rnds. Knit 1 rnd, increase 1 st on each needle–52 sts (13-13-13-13).

Next Rnd: *Needle 1:* Knit to last 2 sts, skp; *Needles 2 and 3:* Knit; *Needle 4:* K2tog, knit to end–64 sts remain.

Decrease Rnd: *Needle 1:* Knit to last 3 sts, skp, k1; *Needles 2 and 3:* Knit; *Needle 4:* K1, k2tog, knit to end–62 sts remain (19-12-12-19). Work even for 1 rnd. Repeat Decrease Rnd every other rnd 7 times–48 sts remain (12 12-12-12).

FOOT

Work even until piece measures 8", or 1½" less than desired length from back of Heel.

TOE

Decrease Rnd: *Needle 1:* Knit to last 3 sts, skp, k1; *Needle 2:* K1, k2tog, knit to end; *Needle 3:* Knit to last 3 sts, skp, k1; *Needle 4:* K1, k2tog, knit to end–44 sts remain. Knit 1 rnd.
Repeat Decrease Rnd every other rnd 3 times, then every rnd 3 times–20 sts remain (5-5-5-5). Knit to end of Needle 1.

FINISHING

Break yarn, leaving long tail. Transfer sts from Needle 1 to Needle 4, and sts from Needle 3 to Needle 2. Using Kitchener st (see General Techniques, page 140), graft Toe sts. Weave in ends. Block lightly.

KEY

☐ **Knit**

⊡ **Purl**

Ⓠ **K1-tbl**

RT: K2tog, but do not drop sts from left-hand needle, insert right-hand needle between 2 sts just worked and knit first st again, slip both sts from left-hand needle together.

LT: Knit into back of second st, then knit first and second sts together through back loops, slip both sts from left-hand needle together.

C3F: Slip next st to cn, hold to front, [k1-tbl] twice, k1-tbl from cn.

C3B: Slip next st to cn, hold to back, [k1-tbl] twice, k1-tbl from cn.

C4B: Slip 2 sts to cn, hold to back, k2, k2 from cn.

C4F: Slip 2 sts to cn, hold to front, k2, k2 from cn.

∽**103**

PATTERN A

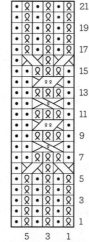

5 3 1

⌊ 6-st repeat ⌋

PATTERN B

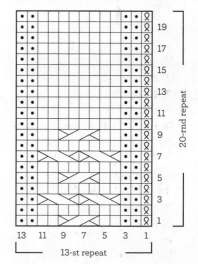

20-rnd repeat

13 11 9 7 5 3 1

13-st repeat

biwa

When I spotted the stitch pattern showcased in these socks, I immediately saw a resemblance between the triangular shape filled with lines of twisted knit stitches and the strings on some musical instruments. After doing some research, I discovered that there is a traditional Japanese short-necked lute—called a *biwa*—that is shaped like this. The *biwa* was played in the seventh century in the imperial court and in early puppet plays. It was also played by blind monk entertainers, the Japanese equivalent of traveling minstrels.

This stitch pattern combines twisted stitches (created by knitting into the back of each stitch) and simple lacework created with yarnovers and two different left-leaning decreases: ssk and skp. While it is unusual in Western patterns to see two different decreases leaning the same way used together, the combination here reflects the attention paid to detail in Japanese knitting: The two varieties of decreases paired together give a very subtle design effect that could easily be overlooked.

FINISHED MEASUREMENTS
7½" Foot circumference
9½" Foot length from back of Heel
8" Leg length to base of Heel

YARN
Crystal Palace Yarns Panda Silk (52% bamboo / 43% superwash merino wool / 5% combed silk; 50 grams / 204 yards) : 2 balls #3021 Mocha

NEEDLES
One set of five double-pointed needles (dpn) size US 1 (2.25 mm)
Change needle size if necessary to obtain correct gauge.

NOTIONS
Stitch marker

GAUGE
32 sts and 46 rnds = 4" (10 cm) in Stockinette stitch (St st)

STITCH PATTERNS

PATTERN A
(multiple of 2 sts; 9-rnd repeat)
Rnds 1 and 5: Knit.
Rnds 2, 4, 6, and 8: Purl.
Rnds 3 and 7: *Ssk, yo; repeat from * to end.
Rnd 9: Knit.

PATTERN B
(multiple of 2 sts; 1-rnd repeat)
All Rnds: *K1, p1; repeat from * to end.

PATTERN C
(multiple of 21 sts)
Rnd 1: *Yo, ssk, p1, k8, skp, [k1-tbl, p1] twice, k1-tbl, yo, p3; repeat from * to end.
Rnd 2: *K2, p9, [k1-tbl] twice, [p1, k1-tbl] twice, p4; repeat from * to end.
Rnd 3: *K2tog, yo, p1, [ssk, yo] 4 times, skp, [p1, k1-tbl] twice, yo, p4; repeat from * to end.
Rnd 4: *K2, p9, [k1-tbl, p1] twice, k1-tbl, p5; repeat from * to end.
Rnd 5: *Yo, ssk, p1, k8, skp, k1-tbl, p1, k1-tbl, yo, p5; repeat from * to end.
Rnd 6: *K2, p9, [k1-tbl] twice, p1, k1-tbl, p6; repeat from * to end.
Rnd 7: *K2tog, yo, p1, [ssk, yo] 4 times, skp, p1, k1-tbl, yo, p6; repeat from * to end.
Rnd 8: *K2, p9, k1-tbl, p1, k1-tbl, p7; repeat from * to end.
Rnd 9: *Yo, ssk, p1, k8, skp, k1-tbl, yo, p7; repeat from * to end.
Rnd 10: *K2, p1, [k1-tbl, p1] 4 times, [k1-tbl] twice, p8; repeat from * to end.
Rnd 11: *K2tog, yo, p1, [k1-tbl, p1] 4 times, skp, yo, p8; repeat from * to end.
Rnd 12: *K2, p1, [k1-tbl, p1] 4 times, k1-tbl, p9; repeat from * to end.
Rnd 13: *Yo, ssk, p1, yo, [k1-tbl, p1] 3 times, k1-tbl, k2tog, p9; repeat from * to end.

Rnd 14: *K2, p2, [k1-tbl, p1] 3 times, [k1-tbl] twice, p9; repeat from * to end.
Rnd 15: *K2tog, yo, p2, yo, [k1-tbl, p1] 3 times, k2tog, p9; repeat from * to end.
Rnd 16: *K2, p3, [k1-tbl, p1] 3 times, k1-tbl, p9; repeat from * to end.
Rnd 17: *Yo, ssk, p3, yo, [k1-tbl, p1] twice, k1-tbl, k2tog, k8, p1; repeat from * to end.
Rnd 18: *K2, p4, [k1-tbl, p1] twice, [k1-tbl] twice, p9; repeat from * to end.
Rnd 19: *K2tog, yo, p4, yo, [k1-tbl, p1] twice, k2tog, [ssk, yo] 4 times, p1; repeat from * to end.
Rnd 20: *K2, p5, [k1-tbl, p1] twice, k1-tbl, p9; repeat from * to end.
Rnd 21: *Yo, ssk, p5, yo, k1-tbl, p1, k1-tbl, k2tog, k8, p1; repeat from * to end.
Rnd 22: *K2, p6, k1-tbl, p1, [k1-tbl] twice, p9; repeat from * to end.
Rnd 23: *K2tog, yo, p6, yo, k1-tbl, p1, k2tog, [ssk, yo] 4 times, p1; repeat from * to end.
Rnd 24: *K2, p7, k1-tbl, p1, k1-tbl, p9; repeat from * to end.
Rnd 25: *Yo, ssk, p7, yo, k1-tbl, k2tog, k8, p1; repeat from * to end.
Rnd 26: *K2, p8, [k1-tbl] twice, [p1, k1-tbl] 4 times, p1; repeat from * to end.
Rnd 27: *K2tog, yo, p8, yo, k2tog, [p1, k1-tbl] 4 times, p1; repeat from * to end.
Rnd 28: *K2, p9, [k1-tbl, p1] 5 times; repeat from * to end.
Rnd 29: *Yo, ssk, p9, skp, [k1-tbl, p1] 3 times, k1-tbl, yo, p1; repeat from * to end.
Rnd 30: *K2, p9, [k1-tbl] twice, [p1, k1-tbl] 3 times, p2; repeat from * to end.
Rnd 31: *K2tog, yo, p9, skp, [p1, k1-tbl] 3 times, yo, p2; repeat from * to end.
Rnd 32: *K2, p9, [k1-tbl, p1] 3 times, k1-tbl, p3; repeat from * to end.

LEG
CO 66 sts. Divide sts evenly among 3 needles (22-22-22). Join for working in the rnd, being careful not to twist sts; place marker (pm) for beginning of rnd. Begin Pattern A; work even for 9 rnds.
Next Rnd: Change to Pattern B; work even for 9 rnds, decreasing 1 st at end of each needle on last rnd–63 sts remain.
Next Rnd: Change to Pattern C; work Rnds 1-32 once, then Rnds 1-24 once.

HEEL FLAP
Set-Up Row 1 (RS): K1, M1, k14, turn–64 sts.
Set-Up Row 2: Slip 1, p31, working all 32 sts onto 1 needle for Heel Flap, and removing marker. Transfer remaining 32 sts to 2 needles (16-16) for instep.
Row 1: Working only on 32 Heel Flap sts, *slip 1, k1; repeat from * to end.
Row 2: Slip 1, purl to end.
Repeat Rows 1 and 2 eleven times.

TURN HEEL
Set-Up Row 1 (RS): Slip 1, k17, skp, k1, turn.
Set-Up Row 2: Slip 1, p5, p2tog, p1, turn.
Row 1: Slip 1, knit to 1 st before gap, skp (the 2 sts on either side of gap), k1, turn.
Row 2: Slip 1, purl to 1 st before gap, p2tog (the 2 sts on either side of gap), p1, turn.
Repeat Rows 1 and 2 five times, omitting final k1 and p1 sts in last repeat of Rows 1 and 2–18 sts remain.

GUSSET
Next Row (RS): *Needle 1:* Knit across Heel Flap sts, pick up and knit 13 sts along left side of Heel Flap, M1; *Needles 2 and 3:* Knit across sts on instep needles;

Needle 4: M1, pick up and knit 13 sts along right side of Heel Flap, k9 from Needle 1. Join for working in the rnd; pm for beginning of rnd–78 sts (23-16-16-23).

Next Rnd: *Needle 1:* Knit to last 2 sts, skp; *Needles 2 and 3:* Knit; *Needle 4:* K2tog, knit to end–76 sts remain.

Decrease Rnd: *Needle 1:* Knit to last 3 sts, skp, k1; *Needles 2 and 3:* Knit; *Needle 4:* K1, k2tog, knit to end–74 sts remain (21-16-16-21). Work even for 1 rnd.

Repeat Decrease Rnd every other rnd 5 times–64 sts remain (16-16-16-16).

FOOT

*****Next Rnd:** *Needle 1:* Knit; *Needles 2 and 3:* Change to Pattern A, beginning with Rnd 2; *Needle 4:* Knit. Work even for 6 rnds.

Next Rnd: Change to St st (knit every rnd) across all needles. Work even for 1¼". Repeat from * once.

Next Rnd: Continuing in St st across all needles, work even until Foot measures 8", or 1½" less than desired length from back of Heel.

TOE

Decrease Rnd: *Needle 1:* Knit to last 3 sts, skp, k1; *Needle 2:* K1, k2tog, knit to end; *Needle 3:* Knit to last 3 sts, skp, k1; *Needle 4:* K1, k2tog, knit to end–60 sts remain. Knit 1 rnd.

Repeat Decrease Rnd every other rnd 10 times–20 sts remain (5-5-5-5). Knit to end of Needle 1.

FINISHING

Break yarn, leaving long tail. Transfer sts from Needle 1 to Needle 4, and sts from Needle 3 to Needle 2. Using Kitchener st (see General Techniques, page 140), graft Toe sts. Weave in ends. Block lightly.

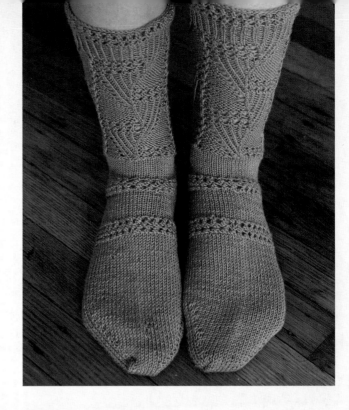

KEY

☐	Knit
•	Purl
ℚ	K1-tbl
O	Yo
╱	K2tog
╲	Skp
⟍	Ssk

PATTERN C

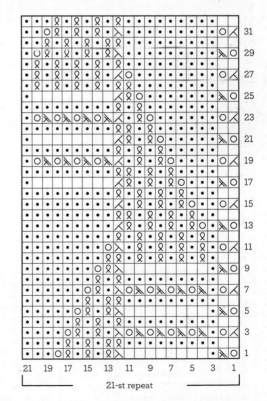

| 21 | 19 | 17 | 15 | 13 | 11 | 9 | 7 | 5 | 3 | 1 |

21-st repeat

kimono

lace

The kimono, which literally means "something to wear," is familiar to most people as the national costume of Japan. This full-length robe, tied with a wide sash called an obi, originated in the seventh century, and it can be very elaborate, composed of up to twenty different layers of embroidered fabrics, each of which has special meaning. In current times, kimonos are worn primarily for ceremonial purposes during weddings, funerals, and special tea ceremonies or flower-arranging demonstrations.

Like the kimonos of old, these Kimono Lace socks are very decorative, composed of multiple design elements. The top has a picot-edged hem, and the lace pattern in the body of the sock, composed of yarnovers and left- and right-leaning decreases, is interrupted periodically by a cablelike pattern that swirls in one direction and then the other. This pattern, while complicated-looking, does not require any complex stitch maneuvers, making it easier to construct than it appears.

FINISHED MEASUREMENTS
8" Foot circumference
10" Foot length from back of Heel
8" Leg length to base of Heel

YARN
elann.com Sock It to Me 4 Ply
(75% superwash wool / 25% nylon; 50 grams / 229 yards): 2 skeins #40453 Rose Wine

NEEDLES
One set of five double-pointed needles (dpn) size US 1 (2.25 mm)
Change needle size if necessary to obtain correct gauge.

NOTIONS
Stitch marker

GAUGE
32 sts and 44 rnds = 4" (10 cm) in Stockinette stitch (St st)

STITCH PATTERNS

PATTERN A

(multiple of 16 sts; 32-rnd repeat)

Rnd 1: *[Ssk, yo] 3 times, k1, p1, yo, k2, ssk, k3, p1; repeat from * to end.

Rnd 2 and All Even-Numbered Rnds: *K7, p1; repeat from * to end.

Rnd 3: *[Ssk, yo] 3 times, k1, p1, k1, yo, k2, ssk, k2, p1; repeat from * to end.

Rnd 5: *[Ssk, yo] 3 times, k1, p1, k2, yo, k2, ssk, k1, p1; repeat from * to end.

Rnd 7: *[Ssk, yo] 3 times, k1, p1, k3, yo, k2, ssk, p1; repeat from * to end.

Rnd 9: *[Ssk, yo] 3 times, k1, p1, yo, k2, ssk, k3, p1; repeat from * to end.

Rnd 11: *[Ssk, yo] 3 times, k1, p1, k1, yo, k2, ssk, k2, p1; repeat from * to end.

Rnd 13: *[Ssk, yo] 3 times, k1, p1, k2, yo, k2, ssk, k1, p1; repeat from * to end.

Rnd 15: *[Ssk, yo] 3 times, k1, p1, k3, yo, k2, ssk, p1; repeat from * to end.

Rnd 17: *K3, k2tog, k2, yo, p1, k1, [yo, k2tog] 3 times, p1; repeat from * to end.

Rnd 19: *K2, k2tog, k2, yo, k1, p1, k1, [yo, k2tog] 3 times, p1; repeat from * to end.

Rnd 21: *K1, k2tog, k2, yo, k2, p1, k1, [yo, k2tog] 3 times, p1; repeat from * to end.

Rnd 23: *K2tog, k2, yo, k3, p1, k1, [yo, k2tog] 3 times, p1; repeat from * to end.

Rnd 25: *K3, k2tog, k2, yo, p1, k1, [yo, k2tog] 3 times, p1; repeat from * to end.

Rnd 27: *K2, k2tog, k2, yo, k1, p1, k1, [yo, k2tog] 3 times, p1; repeat from * to end.

Rnd 29: *K1, k2tog, k2, yo, k2, p1, k1, [yo, k2tog] 3 times, p1; repeat from * to end.

Rnd 31: *K2tog, k2, yo, k3, p1, k1, [yo, k2tog] 3 times, p1; repeat from * to end.

Rnd 32: Repeat Rnd 2.
Repeat Rnds 1-32 for Pattern A.

LEG

CO 64 sts. Divide sts evenly among 4 needles (16-16-16-16). Join for working in the rnd, being careful not to twist sts; place marker (pm) for beginning of rnd. Knit 6 rnds.

Next Rnd (Turning Rnd): *Yo, k2tog; repeat from * to end. Knit 6 rnds.

Next Rnd: Change to Pattern A. Work even until 2 vertical repeats of Pattern A have been completed.

HEEL FLAP

Set-Up Row 1 (RS): K16, turn.
Set-Up Row 2: Slip 1, p31, working all 32 sts onto 1 needle for Heel Flap, and removing marker. Leave remaining 32 sts on 2 needles for instep.
Row 1: Working only on 32 Heel Flap sts, *slip 1, k1; repeat from * to end.
Row 2: Slip 1, purl to end.
Repeat Rows 1 and 2 eleven times.

TURN HEEL

Set-Up Row 1 (RS): Slip 1, k17, skp, k1, turn.
Set-Up Row 2: Slip 1, p5, p2tog, p1, turn.
Row 1: Slip 1, knit to 1 st before gap, skp (the 2 sts on either side of gap), k1, turn.
Row 2: Slip 1, purl to 1 st before gap, p2tog (the 2 sts on either side of gap), p1, turn.
Repeat Rows 1 and 2 five times, omitting final k1 and p1 sts in last repeat of Rows 1 and 2–18 sts remain.

GUSSET

Next Row (RS): *Needle 1:* Knit across Heel Flap sts, pick up and knit 13 sts along left side of Heel Flap, M1; *Needles 2 and 3:* Work even in Pattern A as established; *Needle 4:* M1, pick up and knit 13 sts along right side of Heel Flap, k9 from Needle 1. Join for working in the rnd; pm for beginning of rnd–78 sts (23-16-16-23).

Next Rnd: *Needle 1:* Knit to last 2 sts, skp; *Needles 2 and 3:* Work even as established; *Needle 4:* K2tog, knit to end–76 sts remain.

Decrease Rnd: *Needle 1:* Knit to last 3 sts, skp, k1; *Needles 2 and 3:* Work even as established; *Needle 4:* K1, k2tog, knit to end–74 sts remain (21-16-16-21). Work even for 1 rnd.

Repeat Decrease Rnd every other rnd 5 times–64 sts remain (16-16-16-16).

FOOT

Work even until Rnd 16 of Pattern A is complete.

Next Rnd: Change to St st (knit every rnd) across all sts; work even until Foot measures 8½", or 1½" less than desired length from back of Heel.

TOE

Decrease Rnd: *Needle 1:* Knit to last 3 sts, skp, k1; *Needle 2:* K1, k2tog, knit to end; *Needle 3:* Knit to last 3 sts, skp, k1; *Needle 4:* K1, k2tog, knit to end–60 sts remain. Knit 2 rnds.

Repeat Decrease Rnd every 3 rnds twice, every other rnd 5 times, then every rnd 3 times–20 sts remain (5-5-5-5). Knit to end of Needle 1.

FINISHING

Break yarn, leaving long tail. Transfer sts from Needle 1 to Needle 4, and sts from Needle 3 to Needle 2. Using Kitchener st (see General Techniques, page 140), graft Toe sts. Fold CO edge to WS at Turning Rnd and sew in place, being careful not to let sts show on RS. Weave in ends. Block lightly.

KEY

☐ Knit

⊡ Purl

⊙ Yo

◩ K2tog

◪ Ssk

PATTERN A

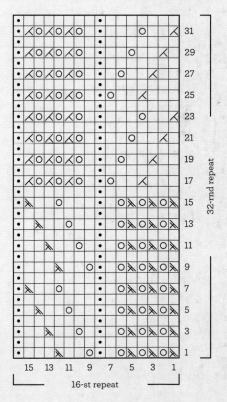

32-rnd repeat

16-st repeat

kaiso

The lace design and fluid bands of this pattern look to me as if they could be moving under water, like seaweed. The Japanese word for seaweed is *kaiso*, and varieties of it have been used for centuries in Japanese cooking.

This sock design is a very simple one, using only knits, purls, yarnovers, and decreases to create a lace pattern that is reminiscent of the feather and fan design familiar to many Western knitters. Here, it has been simplified and modified with garter bands that add a rhythmic feel as they flow up and down. The soft, pale yellow-green bamboo yarn further reflects the color and fluid feel of certain types of seaweed.

FINISHED MEASUREMENTS
7" Foot circumference
9¼" Foot length from back of Heel
8¾" Leg length to base of Heel, unrolled

YARN
S.R. Kertzer On Your Toes Bamboo
(75% bamboo / 25% nylon; 100 grams / 328 yards): 1 skein #ON260318
Rainforest Dew

NEEDLES
One set of five double-pointed needles (dpn) size US 2 (2.75 mm)
Change needle size if necessary to obtain correct gauge.

NOTIONS
Stitch marker

GAUGE
26 sts and 38 rnds = 4" (10 cm) in Stockinette stitch (St st)

Row 1: Working only on 24 Heel Flap sts, *slip 1, k1; repeat from * to end.
Row 2: Slip 1, purl to end.
Repeat Rows 1 and 2 eleven times.

TURN HEEL

Set-Up Row 1 (RS): Slip 1, k13, skp, k1, turn.
Set-Up Row 2: Slip 1, p5, p2tog, p1, turn.
Row 1: Slip 1, knit to 1 st before gap, skp (the 2 sts on either side of gap), k1, turn.
Row 2: Slip 1, purl to 1 st before gap, p2tog (the 2 sts on either side of gap), p1, turn.
Repeat Rows 1 and 2 three times, omitting the final k1 and p1 in the last repeat of Rows 1 and 2–14 sts remain.

GUSSET

Next Row (RS): *Needle 1:* Knit across Heel Flap sts, pick up and knit 13 sts along left side of Heel Flap, M1; *Needles 2 and 3:* Work even in Pattern A as established; *Needle 4:* M1, pick up and knit 13 sts along right side of Heel Flap, k7 from Needle 1. Join for working in the rnd; pm for beginning of rnd–66 sts (21-12-12-21).
Next Rnd: *Needle 1:* Knit to last 2 sts, skp; *Needles 2 and 3:* Work even as established; *Needle 4:* K2tog, knit to end–64 sts remain.

STITCH PATTERN

PATTERN A
(multiple of 12 sts; 22-rnd repeat)
Rnds 1, 2, 4, 6, 8, 10, 12, and 15-18: Knit.
Rnds 3, 7, and 11: *[K2tog] twice, [yo, k1] 3 times, yo, [ssk] twice, k1; repeat from * to end.
Rnds 5 and 9: *K2tog, k2, yo, k3, yo, k2, ssk, k1; repeat from * to end.
Rnds 13, 14, 19, and 20: Purl.
Rnds 21 and 22: Knit.
Repeat Rnds 1-22 for Pattern A.

LEG

CO 48 sts. Divide sts evenly among 4 needles (12-12-12-12). [Knit 1 rnd, purl 1 rnd] twice.
Next Rnd: Begin Pattern A; work Rnds 1-22 twice, then rnds 1-20 once.

HEEL FLAP

Set-Up Row 1 (RS): K12, turn.
Set-Up Row 2: Slip 1, p23, working all 24 sts onto 1 needle for Heel Flap, and removing marker. Leave remaining 24 sts on 2 needles for instep.

Decrease Rnd: *Needle 1:* Knit to last 3 sts, skp, k1; *Needles 2 and 3:* Work even as established; *Needle 4:* K1, k2tog, knit to end–62 sts remain (19-12-12-19). Work even for 1 rnd.

Repeat Decrease Rnd every other rnd 7 times–48 sts remain (12-12-12-12).

FOOT

Work even until Foot measures 7¾", or 1½" less than desired length from back of Heel.

TOE

Decrease Rnd: *Needle 1:* Knit to last 3 sts, skp, k1; *Needle 2:* K1, k2tog, knit to end; *Needle 3:* Knit to last 3 sts, skp, k1; *Needle 4:* K1, k2tog, knit to end–44 sts remain. Knit 1 rnd.

Repeat Decrease Rnd every other rnd 3 times, then every rnd 3 times–20 sts remain (5-5-5-5). Knit to end of Needle 1.

FINISHING

Break yarn, leaving long tail. Transfer sts from Needle 1 to Needle 4, and sts from Needle 3 to Needle 2. Using Kitchener st (see General Techniques, page 140), graft Toe sts. Weave in ends. Block lightly.

KEY

☐ Knit
⊡ Purl
⊙ Yo
◹ K2tog
◺ Ssk

PATTERN A

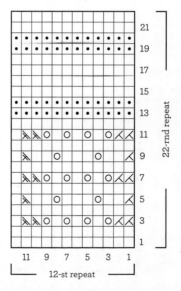

tatami

These socks are named after the woven straw matting called tatami that is used as a floor covering in Japan. The main stitch pattern of this sock, while obviously knitted, looks woven. Today tatami are quite common in Japan, but when they originated in the seventh century, they were a luxury reserved for the wealthy; the lower classes covered their dirt floors with fabric mats. The tatami had two layers filled with rice straw and decorative fabric bindings.

In this pattern—one of the least complicated in this book—the woven "tatami" effect in the body of the sock is created with a simple six-stitch and eight-round repeat that requires only knits, purls, and the center double decrease. I sized my Tatami socks for adults and children. Both versions are worked from the cuff down, but on the adult version, the tatami stitch pattern is repeated twice on the instep. On the child's, it is repeated only once since the foot is much shorter.

SIZES
Child (Adult)

FINISHED MEASUREMENTS
5½ (7½)" Foot circumference
6 (9¾)" Foot length from back of Heel
5½ (10)" Leg length to base of Heel

YARN
SR Kertzer On Your Toes Bamboo
(75% bamboo / 25% nylon; 100 grams /
328 yards): 1 skein #ON260805
Seashell Multi

NEEDLES
One set of five double-pointed needles
(dpn) size 2 (2.75 mm)
Change needle size if necessary to obtain
correct gauge.

NOTIONS
Stitch marker

GAUGE
25 sts and 38 rnds = 4" (10 cm) in
Stockinette stitch (St st)

STITCH PATTERNS

PATTERN A (Child only)
(multiple of 4 sts)
Rnds 1-4 and 6: *K2, p2; repeat from * to end.
Rnd 5: *K2tog, yo, p2; repeat from * to end.
Rnd 7: *Yo, ssk, p2; repeat from * to end.
Rnds 8-11: Repeat Rnd 1.

PATTERN B (Adult only)
(multiple of 4 sts)
Rnds 1-4, 6, 8, and 10: *K2, p2; repeat from * to end.
Rnds 5 and 9: *K2tog, yo, p2; repeat from * to end.
Rnds 7 and 11: *Yo, ssk, p2; repeat from * to end.
Rnds 12-14: Repeat Rnd 1.

PATTERN C
(multiple of 6 sts; 8-rnd repeat)
Rnd 1: *K3, yo, s2kp2, yo; repeat from * to end.
Rnds 2, 3, and 4: *K3, p3; repeat from * to end.
Rnd 5: *Yo, s2kp2, yo, k3; repeat from * to end.
Rnds 6-8: *P3, k3; repeat from * to end.
Repeat Rnds 1-8 for Pattern C.

LEG

CO 36 (48) sts. Divide sts evenly among 4 needles [9-9-9-9 (12-12-12-12)]. Join for working in the rnd, being careful not to twists sts; place marker (pm) for beginning of rnd. Begin Pattern A (B); work even for 11 (14) rnds. Knit 1 rnd.
Next Rnd: Change to Pattern C; work even until piece measures 4¼(8)" from the beginning, ending with Rnd 4 or 8 of Pattern C.

HEEL FLAP

Set-Up Row 1 (RS): K9 (12), turn.
Set-Up Row 2: Slip 1, p17 (23), working all 18 (24) sts onto 1 needle for Heel Flap, and removing marker. Leave remaining 18 (24) sts on 2 needles for instep.
Row 1: Working only on 18 (24) Heel Flap sts, *slip 1, k1; repeat from * to end.
Row 2: Slip 1, purl to end.
Repeat Rows 1 and 2 seven (ten) times.

TURN HEEL

Set-Up Row 1 (RS): Slip 1, k10 (13), skp, k1, turn.
Set-Up Row 2: Slip 1, p5, p2tog, p1, turn.
Row 1: Slip 1, knit to 1 st before gap, skp (the 2 sts on either side of gap), k1, turn.
Row 2: Slip 1, purl to 1 st before gap, p2tog (the 2 sts on either side of gap), p1, turn.
Repeat Rows 1 and 2 one (three) time(s), omitting final k1 and p1 sts in last repeat of Rows 1 and 2–12 (14) sts remain.

GUSSET

Next Rnd: *Needle 1:* Knit across Heel Flap sts, pick up and knit 9 (12) sts along left side of Heel Flap, M1; *Needles 2 and 3:* Knit across sts on instep needles; *Needle 4:* M1, pick up and knit 9 (12) sts along right side of Heel Flap, k5 (7) from Needle 1. Join for working in the rnd; pm for beginning of rnd–50 (64) sts [16-9-9-16 (20-12-12-20)].

Next Rnd: *Needle 1:* Knit to last 2 sts, skp; *Needles 2 and 3:* Knit across sts on instep needles; *Needle 4:* K2tog, knit to end–48 (62) sts remain.

Decrease Rnd: *Needle 1:* Knit to last 3 sts, skp, k1; *Needles 2 and 3:* Knit; *Needle 4:* K1, k2tog, knit to end–46 (60) sts remain [14-9-9-14 (18-12-12-18)]. Work even for 1 rnd. Repeat Decrease Rnd every other rnd 5 (6) times–36 (48) sts remain [9-9-9-9 (12-12-12-12)].

CHILD SIZE ONLY
AT THE SAME TIME, when 12 sts remain on Needles 1 and 4, continuing with Gusset decreases on Needles 1 and 4 as established, change to Pattern C across Needles 2 and 3.

FOOT

CHILD SIZE ONLY
Work even until 1 vertical repeat of Pattern C has been completed. Change to St st (knit all rnds) across all needles. Work even until Foot measures 4¾", or 1¼" less than desired length from back of Heel.

ADULT SIZE ONLY
*Next Rnd: *Needle 1:* Knit; *Needles 2 and 3:* Change to Pattern C; *Needle 4:* Knit. Work even until 1 vertical repeat of Pattern C has been completed.*
Next Rnd: Change to St st. Work even for 1¾".
Repeat from * to * once. Change to St st. Work even until Foot measures 8¼", or 1½" less than desired length from Back of Heel.

KEY

☐ Knit
⊡ Purl
Ⓞ Yo
◩ K2tog
◪ Ssk
⩙ S2kp2

PATTERN A

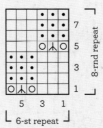

4-st repeat

PATTERN B

4-st repeat

PATTERN C

8-rnd repeat

6-st repeat

TOE

Decrease Rnd: *Needle 1:* Knit to last 3 sts, skp, k1; *Needle 2:* K1, k2tog, knit to end; *Needle 3:* Knit to last 3 sts, skp, k1; *Needle 4:* K1, k2tog, knit to end–32 (44) sts remain. Knit 1 rnd. Repeat Decrease Rnd every other rnd 3 times, then every rnd 0 (3) times–20 sts remain (5-5-5-5). Knit to end of Needle 1.

FINISHING

Break yarn, leaving long tail. Transfer sts from Needle 1 to Needle 4, and sts from Needle 3 to Needle 2. Using Kitchener st (see General Techniques, page 140), graft Toe sts. Weave in ends. Block lightly.

∽ 119

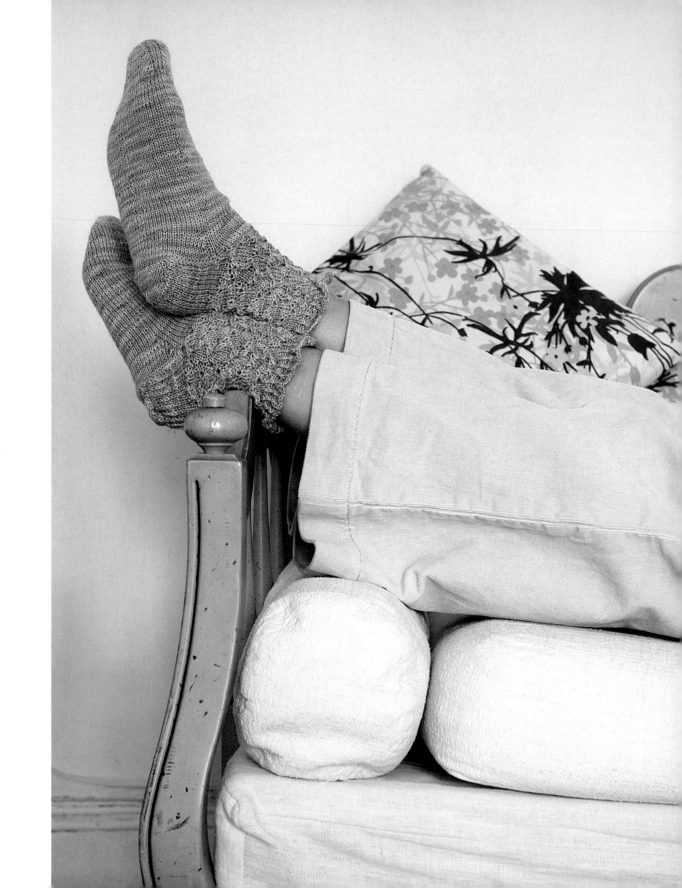

sensu

The *sensu*, or Japanese folding fan, was once an indispensable article for the Japanese people, a portable and beautiful way to create a cooling breeze. Originally quite plain and practical, over time these fans became highly decorated with elegant painting and gold and silver foil—a combination of function and beauty. The opportunity to use a *sensu* has slowly disappeared over the years because of the electric fan and air conditioners, but it is still considered a fine gift item, popular for weddings and anniversaries.

When I saw this stitch pattern originally, it appeared to have a fanlike movement to it that called the *sensu* to mind. As I designed the sock, I added a ruffled edge that seemed to complement the swirling movement of the design. The Sensu sock features a short but decorative leg and a solid, durable foot that showcases a hand-dyed yarn—a modern combination of function and beauty.

FINISHED MEASUREMENTS
7½" Foot circumference
10" Foot length from back of Heel
6½" Leg length to base of Heel, unrolled

YARN
Schaefer Yarn Company Anne
(60% superwash merino wool / 25% mohair / 15% nylon; 4 ounces / 560 yards): 1 hank Green Jeans

NEEDLES
One set of five double-pointed needles (dpn) size US 1 (2.25 mm)
Change needle size if necessary to obtain correct gauge.

NOTIONS
Stitch marker

GAUGE
31 sts and 42 rnds = 4" (10 cm) in Stockinette stitch (St st)

☐ Knit

⊡ Purl

◉ Yo

⧄ Ssk

⧅ K2tog

PATTERN B

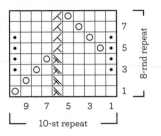

8-rnd repeat

9 7 5 3 1

10-st repeat

STITCH PATTERNS

PATTERN A
(multiple of 2 sts; 1-rnd repeat)
All Rnds: *K1-tbl, p1; repeat from * to end.

PATTERN B
(multiple of 10 sts; 8-rnd repeat)
Rnd 1: *K5, ssk, k3, yo; repeat from * to end.
Rnd 2: *K5, ssk, k2, yo, k1; repeat from * to end.
Rnd 3: *P1, k4, ssk, k1, yo, k1, p1; repeat from * to end.
Rnd 4: *P1, k4, ssk, yo, k2, p1; repeat from * to end.
Rnd 5: *P1, yo, k3, k2tog, k3, p1; repeat from * to end.
Rnd 6: *P1, k1, yo, k2, k2tog, k3, p1; repeat from * to end.
Rnd 7: *K3, yo, k1, k2tog, k4; repeat from * to end.
Rnd 8: *K4, yo, k2tog, k4; repeat from * to end.
Repeat Rnds 1–8 for Pattern B.

LEG

CO 120 sts. Divide sts evenly among 3 needles (40-40-40). Join for working in the rnd, being careful not to twist sts; place marker (pm) for beginning of rnd. Knit 3 rnds.
Decrease Rnd: *K2tog-tbl, p2tog; repeat from * to end–60 sts remain (20-20-20).
Next Rnd: Change to Pattern A; work even for 3 rnds.
Next Rnd: Change to Pattern B; work even until piece measures 4¼" from the beginning, unrolled. Redistribute sts among 4 needles (15-15-15-15).

HEEL FLAP

Set-Up Row 1 (RS): K15.
Set-Up Row 2: Slip 1, p29, working all 30 sts onto 1 needle for Heel Flap, and removing marker. Leave remaining 30 sts on 2 needles for instep.

Row 1: Working only on 30 Heel Flap sts, *slip 1, k1; repeat from * to end.
Row 2: Slip 1, purl to end.
Repeat Rows 1 and 2 eleven times.

TURN HEEL

Set-Up Row 1 (RS): Slip 1, k16, skp, k1, turn.
Set-Up Row 2: Slip 1, p5, p2tog, p1, turn.
Row 1: Slip 1, knit to 1 st before gap, skp (the 2 sts on either side of gap), k1, turn.
Row 2: Slip 1, purl to 1 st before gap, p2tog (the 2 sts on either side of gap), p1, turn.
Repeat Rows 1 and 2 four times–18 sts remain.

GUSSET

Next Row (RS): *Needle 1:* Knit across Heel Flap sts, pick up and knit 13 sts along left side of Heel Flap, M1; *Needles 2 and 3:* Knit across sts on instep needles; *Needle 4:* M1, pick up and knit 13 sts along right side of Heel Flap, k8 from Needle 1. Join for working in the rnd; pm for beginning of rnd–76 sts (23-15-15-23).

Next Rnd: *Needle 1:* Knit to last 2 sts, skp; *Needles 2 and 3:* Knit; *Needle 4:* K2tog, knit to end–74 sts remain.

Decrease Rnd: *Needle 1:* Knit to last 3 sts, skp, k1; *Needles 2 and 3:* Knit; *Needle 4:* K1, k2tog, knit to end–72 sts remain (21-15-15-21). Work even for 1 rnd.

Repeat Decrease Rnd every other rnd 6 times–60 sts remain (15-15-15-15).

FOOT

Work even until Foot measures 8½", or 1½" less than desired length from back of Heel.

TOE

Decrease Rnd: *Needle 1:* Knit to last 3 sts, skp, k1; *Needle 2:* K1, k2tog, knit to end; *Needle 3:* Knit to last 3 sts, skp, k1; *Needle 4:* K1, k2tog, knit to end–56 sts remain. Knit 1 rnd.

Repeat Decrease Rnd every other rnd 9 times–20 sts remain (5-5-5-5). Knit to end of Needle 1.

FINISHING

Break yarn, leaving long tail. Transfer sts from Needle 1 to Needle 4, and sts from Needle 3 to Needle 2. Using Kitchener st (see General Techniques, page 140), graft Toe sts. Weave in ends. Block lightly.

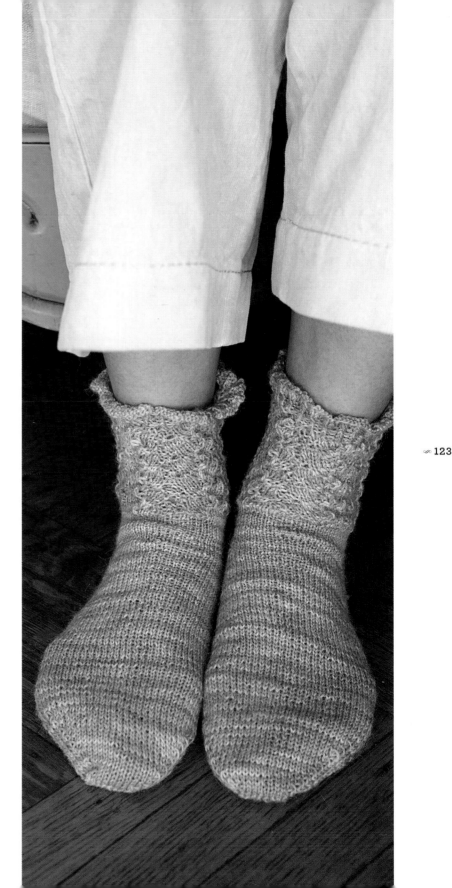

karaoke

The Japanese import karaoke has become a popular form of entertainment in the West, after having become well established in Japan as a way to unwind after a long workday. Some reports say it was invented by a popular Japanese drummer who was asked to provide recordings of his music so others could sing along. Another story says it began when a scheduled singer didn't show up at a snack bar in Kobe, and the audience took turns singing to recorded music instead. Either way, karaoke is born out of a Japanese love of music and singing.

The Karaoke knee socks "sing" to me with their perky bobbles, pkoks, and stitches moving to the right and left. It is not a difficult pattern—lending confidence to knitters still developing their sock-making ability—but provides a lovely rhythmic movement within the sock itself.

Finished Measurements
7½" Foot circumference
9½" Foot length from back of Heel
16¾" Leg length to base of Heel

Yarn
Lorna's Laces Shepherd Sport
(100% superwash wool; 2.6 ounces / 200 yards): 2 hanks #4ns Blackberry.
Note: If you work the Foot longer than 9½" from back of Heel, you will need to purchase an additional hank.

Needles
One 16" (40 cm) long circular (circ) needle size US 3 (3.25 mm)
One set of five double-pointed needles (dpn) size US 3 (3.25 mm)
Change needle size if necessary to obtain correct gauge.

Notions
Stitch marker

Gauge
26 sts and 34 rnds = 4" (10 cm) in Stockinette stitch (St st)

Abbreviations
Pkok: Slip third st on left-hand needle over first 2 sts and off needle; k1, yo, k1 (see page 12).
RT: K2tog, but do not drop sts from left-hand needle, insert right-hand needle between 2 sts just worked and knit first st again, slip both sts from left-hand needle together.
LT: Knit into back of second st, then knit first and second sts together through back loops, slip both sts from left-hand needle together.
MB (Make Bobble): Knit into front, back, front, back, then front of next st to increase to 5 sts; pass second, third, fourth, then fifth st over first st and off needle.

STITCH PATTERNS

PATTERN A
(multiple of 2 sts; 1-rnd repeat)

All Rnds: *K1-tbl, p1; repeat from * to end.

PATTERN B
(multiple of 17 sts; 28-rnd repeat)

Rnd 1: *P1, pkok, p3, k6, k2tog, yo, p2; repeat from * to end.

Rnds 2, 4, 6, 8, 10, and 12: *P1, k3, p3, k8, p2; repeat from * to end.

Rnd 3: *P1, k3, p3, k5, k2tog, k1, yo, p2; repeat from * to end.

Rnd 5: *P1, pkok, p3, k4, k2tog, k2, yo, p2; repeat from * to end.

Rnd 7: *P1, k3, p3, k3, k2tog, k3, yo, p2; repeat from * to end.

Rnd 9: *P1, pkok, p3, k2, k2tog, k4, yo, p2; repeat from * to end.

Rnd 11: *P1, k3, p3, k1, k2tog, k5, yo, p2; repeat from * to end.

Rnd 13: *P1, pkok, p3, k2tog, MB, k5, yo, p2; repeat from * to end.

Rnd 14: *P1, k1, k1-tbl, k1, p3, k1, k1-tbl, k6, p2; repeat from * to end.

Rnd 15: *RT, k1-tbl, LT, p2, yo, ssk, k6, p2; repeat from * to end.

Rnds 16, 18, 20, 22, 24, and 26: *[K1-tbl, p1] twice, k1-tbl, p2, k8, p2; repeat from * to end.

Rnd 17: *[K1-tbl, p1] twice, k1-tbl, p2, yo, k1, ssk, k5, p2; repeat from * to end.

Rnd 19: *[K1-tbl, p1] twice, k1-tbl, p2, yo, k2, ssk, k4, p2; repeat from * to end.

Rnd 21: *[K1-tbl, p1] twice, k1-tbl, p2, yo, k3, ssk, k3, p2; repeat from * to end.

Rnd 23: *[K1-tbl, p1] twice, k1-tbl, p2, yo, k4, ssk, k2, p2; repeat from * to end.

Rnd 25: *[K1-tbl, p1] twice, k1-tbl, p2, yo, k5, ssk, k1, p2; repeat from * to end.

Rnd 27: *LT, k1-tbl, RT, p2, yo, k5, MB, ssk, p2; repeat from * to end.

Rnd 28: *P1, [k1-tbl] 3 times, p3, k8, p2; repeat from * to end.

Repeat Rnds 1-28 for Pattern B.

LEG

Note: Change to dpn when necessary for number of sts on needle.

Using circ needle, CO 84 sts. Join for working in the rnd, being careful not to twist sts; place marker (pm) for beginning of rnd. Begin Pattern A; work even for 14 rnds, increase 1 st on last rnd–85 sts.

Next Rnd: K17, pm, work Pattern B over 51 sts, pm, knit to end. Work even for 5 rnds.

Shape Calf: Continuing in pattern as established, decrease 2 sts this rnd, every 7 rnds 10 times, then every 4 rnds 5 times, as follows: Work to 2 sts before marker, k2tog, work to next marker, skp, work to end–53 sts remain. Work even until 3 vertical repeats of Pattern B have been completed, then work Rnds 1-14 once. Knit 1 rnd, decrease 5 sts evenly–48 sts remain. Redistribute sts evenly among 4 needles (12-12-12-12).

HEEL FLAP

Set-Up Row 1 (RS): K12, turn.

Set-Up Row 2: Slip 1, p23, working all 24 sts onto 1 needle for Heel Flap, and removing marker. Leave remaining 24 sts on 2 needles for instep.

Row 1: Working only on 24 Heel Flap sts, *slip 1, k1; repeat from * to end.

Row 2: Slip 1, purl to end.

Repeat Rows 1 and 2 eleven times.

TURN HEEL

Set-Up Row 1 (RS): Slip 1, k13, skp, k1, turn.

Set-Up Row 2: Slip 1, p5, p2tog, p1, turn.

Row 1: Slip 1, knit to 1 st before gap, skp (the 2 sts on either side of gap), k1, turn.

Row 2: Slip 1, purl to 1 st before gap, p2tog (the 2 sts on either side of gap), p1, turn.

Repeat Rows 1 and 2 three times, omitting final k1 and p1 sts in last repeat of Rows 1 and 2–14 sts remain.

GUSSET

Next Row (RS): *Needle 1:* Knit across Heel Flap sts, pick up and knit 13 sts along left side of Heel Flap, M1; *Needles 2 and 3:* Knit across sts on instep needles; *Needle 4:* M1, pick up and knit 13 sts along right side of Heel Flap, k7 from Needle 1. Join for working in the rnd; pm for beginning of rnd–66 sts (21-12-12-21).
Next Rnd: *Needle 1:* Knit to last 2 sts, skp; *Needles 2 and 3:* Knit; *Needle 4:* K2tog, knit to end–64 sts.
Decrease Rnd: *Needle 1:* Knit to last 3 sts, skp, k1; *Needles 2 and 3:* Knit; *Needle 4:* K1, k2tog, knit to end–62 sts (19-12-12-19). Work even for 1 rnd.
Repeat Decrease Rnd every other rnd 7 times–48 sts remain (12-12-12-12).

FOOT

Work even until piece measures 8", or 1½" less than desired length from back of Heel

TOE

Decrease Rnd: *Needle 1:* Knit to last 3 sts, skp, k1; *Needle 2:* K1, k2tog, knit to end; *Needle 3:* Knit to last 3 sts, skp, k1; *Needle 4:* K1, k2tog, knit to end–44 sts remain. Knit 1 rnd.
Repeat Decrease Rnd every other rnd 3 times, then every rnd 3 times–20 sts remain (5-5-5-5). Knit to end of Needle 1.

FINISHING

Break yarn, leaving long tail. Transfer sts from Needle 1 to Needle 4, and sts from Needle 3 to Needle 2. Using Kitchener st (see General Techniques, page 140), graft Toe sts. Weave in ends. Block lightly.

KEY

- ☐ **Knit**
- ⊡ **Purl**
- **K1-tbl**
- ⊙ **Yo**
- ◹ **K2tog**
- ◺ **Ssk**
- ● **MB:** Knit into front, back, front, back, then front of next st to increase to 5 sts; pass second, third, fourth, then fifth st, 1 at a time, over first st and off needle.
- **Pkok:** Slip third st on left-hand needle over first 2 sts and off needle; k1, yo, k1 (see page 12).
- **RT:** K2tog, but do not drop sts from left-hand needle, insert right-hand needle between 2 sts just worked and knit first st again, slip both sts from left-hand needle together.
- **LT:** Knit into back of second st, then knit first and second sts together through back loops, slip both sts from left-hand needle together.

PATTERN B

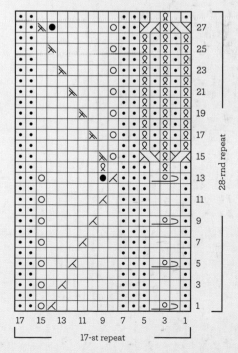

katsura

When I spotted the chart for this stitch pattern in one of my Japanese stitch books, I immediately thought of a tree leaf. I named the socks after the *katsura*, a variety of Japanese ornamental tree known for its delicate leaves, its brilliant red and orange autumnal color, and its scent, which is reminiscent of caramel or cotton candy. In a departure from my usual sock-construction technique, I decided to work these simple socks from the toe up so that I could watch the leaves and stems develop as they do in nature—from the ground up—while I twisted stitches right and left. Like many Japanese stitch patterns, this one seems to have an intrinsic rhythm built into it: As you work the pattern, a portion of a leaf or stem "branches out" to become another leaf or stem—and another, and another—as if the pattern were growing in front of you. The twisted stitches give the leaves a delicate look—like those on the *katsura*—but not too lacy or feminine, making these socks suitable for either men or women.

FINISHED MEASUREMENTS
8" Foot circumference
11" Foot length from back of Heel
10" Leg length to base of Heel

YARN
Regia 4-ply Wool (75% superwash wool / 25% polyamide; 50 grams / 230 yards): 2 skeins #2070 Birch

NEEDLES
One set of five double-pointed needles (dpn) size US 1 (2.25 mm)
Change needle size if necessary to obtain correct gauge.

NOTIONS
Stitch marker

GAUGE
28 sts and 41 rnds = 4" (10 cm) in Stockinette stitch (St st)

ABBREVIATIONS
RT: K2tog, but do not drop sts from left-hand needle, insert right-hand needle between 2 sts just worked and knit first st again, slip both sts from left-hand needle together.
LT: Knit into back of second st, then knit first and second sts together through back loops, slip both sts from left-hand needle together.

Rnd 19: *LT, p5, k1-tbl, p2, [LT] 3 times, p1; repeat from * to end.

Rnd 20: *[K1-tbl] twice, p5, k1-tbl, p3, [k1-tbl, p1] 3 times; repeat from * to end.

Repeat Rnds 1-20 for Pattern A.

TOE

Note: Sock is worked from the toe up. Holding 2 needles parallel, and using Long-Tail CO (see General Techniques, page 141), *CO 1 st on back needle, then 1 st on front needle; repeat from * 9 times, turn–20 sts (10-10).

Next Rnd: Using third needle, *k1-tbl; repeat from * across front needle, then across back needle, joining to work in the rnd; place marker (pm) for beginning of rnd.

Increase Rnd 1: *Needle 1:* K1, M1-r, knit to last st, M1-l, k1; *Needle 2:* Work as for Needle 1–24 sts. Work even for 1 rnd. Redistribute sts among 4 needles (6-6-6-6).

Increase Rnd 2: *Needle 4:* K1, M1-r, knit to end, reposition marker for beginning of rnd; *Needle 1:* Knit to last st, M1-l, k1; *Needle 2:* K1, M1-r, knit to end; *Needle 3:* Knit to last st, M1-l, k1; knit to end of Needle 4–28 sts.

Repeat Increase Rnd 2 every other rnd 9 times–64 sts (16-16-16-16). Work even for 1 rnd. Redistribute sts (15-17-17-15).

FOOT

Next Rnd: *Needle 1:* Knit; *Needles 2 and 3:* Work Pattern A over 34 sts; *Needle 4:* Knit. Work even until Foot measures 9", or 2" less than desired length from Toe. Transfer sts from Needle 1 to Needle 4 for Heel, removing marker. Leave remaining 34 sts on 2 needles for instep.

STITCH PATTERNS

PATTERN A
(multiple of 17 sts; 20-rnd repeat)

Rnd 1: *RT, p5, LT, p2, [LT] twice, p2; repeat from * to end.

Rnd 2: *[K1-tbl] twice, p5, [k1-tbl] twice, p3, k1-tbl, p1, k1-tbl, p2; repeat from * to end.

Rnd 3: *LT, p4, RT, LT, p2, LT, p3; repeat from * to end.

Rnd 4: *[K1-tbl] twice, p4, k1-tbl, p1, [k1-tbl] twice, p3, k1-tbl, p3; repeat from * to end.

Rnd 5: *RT, p3, [RT] twice, LT, p6; repeat from * to end.

Rnd 6: *[K1-tbl] twice, p3, [k1-tbl, p1] twice, [k1-tbl] twice, p6; repeat from * to end.

Rnd 7: *LT, p2, [RT] 3 times, LT, p5; repeat from * to end.

Rnd 8: *[K1-tbl] twice, p2, [k1-tbl, p1] twice, k1-tbl, p2, k1-tbl, p5; repeat from * to end.

Rnd 9: *RT, p1, [RT] 3 times, p2, k1-tbl, p5; repeat from * to end.

Rnd 10: *[K1-tbl] twice, [p1, k1-tbl] 3 times, p3, k1-tbl, p5; repeat from * to end.

Rnd 11: *LT, p2, [RT] twice, p2, RT, p5; repeat from * to end.

Rnd 12: *[K1-tbl] twice, p2, k1-tbl, p1, k1-tbl, p3, [k1-tbl] twice, p5; repeat from * to end.

Rnd 13: *RT, p3, RT, p2, RT, LT, p4; repeat from * to end.

Rnd 14: *[K1-tbl] twice, p3, k1-tbl, p3, [k1-tbl] twice, p1, k1-tbl, p4; repeat from * to end.

Rnd 15: *LT, p6, RT, [LT] twice, p3; repeat from * to end.

Rnd 16: *[K1-tbl] twice, p6, [k1-tbl] twice, [p1, k1-tbl] twice, p3; repeat from * to end.

Rnd 17: *RT, p5, RT, [LT] 3 times, p2; repeat from * to end.

Rnd 18: *[K1-tbl] twice, p5, k1-tbl, p2, [k1-tbl, p1] twice, k1-tbl, p2; repeat from * to end.

HEEL

Note: Heel is shaped using Short Rows (see General Techniques, page 141).

Short Rows 1 (RS) and 2 (WS): Working only on 30 Heel sts, knit to last st, wrp-t; purl to last st, wrp-t.

Short Rows 3 and 4: Knit to 1 st before wrapped st from row below previous row, wrp-t; purl to 1 st before wrapped st from row below previous row, wrp-t.

Repeat Short Rows 3 and 4 until 10 sts remain unworked in the center of the Heel.

Short Rows 5 and 6: Knit to first wrapped st from row below previous row, work wrap together with wrapped st, turn; purl to first wrapped st from row below previous row, work wrap together with wrapped st, turn.

Repeat Short Rows 5 and 6 until all Heel sts have been worked.

Next Row (RS): K15, pm for new beginning of rnd.

LEG

Next Rnd: *Needle 1:* K7, M1, k8, M1; *Needles 2 and 3:* Work even in Pattern A as established; *Needle 4:* M1, k7, M1, k8–68 sts (17-17-17-17).

Next Rnd: Work in Pattern A across all sts. Work even until Leg measures 7½" from end of Short Row Heel shaping, decrease 1 st on each needle on last rnd, working decrease as p2tog within purl section of Pattern A–64 sts remain (16-16-16-16). Make note of # of last rnd of Pattern A worked.

Next Rnd: Work sts 1 and 2 of Pattern A, beginning with rnd of Pattern following last rnd worked, p2, *work sts 1 and 2, p2; repeat from * to end. Work even for 1½". BO all sts loosely in pattern. Weave in ends. Block lightly.

KEY

☐ **Knit**

· **Purl**

Ⴒ **K1-tbl**

▱ **RT:** K2tog, but do not drop sts from left-hand needle, insert right-hand needle between 2 sts just worked and knit first st again, slip both sts from left-hand needle together.

▱ **LT:** Knit into back of second st, then knit first and second sts together through back loops, slip both sts from left-hand needle together.

PATTERN A

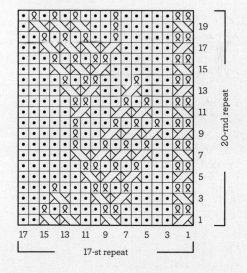

17-st repeat

20-rnd repeat

sumo
slipper

Japan is the only country where sumo wrestling is a professional sport, and its participants are famously known for their great heft, which is instrumental in forcing their opponents out of a circular ring or to touch the ground with any body part other than the soles of their feet—both of which are grounds for victory.

These slipper socks got their name because of the very heavy, organic movement of the cables in this very thick yarn. The pattern integrates stitches twisted to the right and the left and also intertwined into cables. Because of their heft, they likely won't fit into shoes—but they'll do beautifully as slippers around the house.

FINISHED MEASUREMENTS
11" Foot circumference
10" Foot length from back of Heel
9" Leg length to base of Heel

YARN
Lion Brand Wool-Ease Thick and Quick (80% acrylic / 20% wool; 6 ounces / 106 yards) 2 skeins #640-178 Cilantro

NEEDLES
One set of five double-pointed needles (dpn) size US 9 (5.5 mm)
Change needle size if necessary to obtain correct gauge.

NOTIONS
Stitch marker; cable needle (cn)

GAUGE
12 sts and 19 rnds = 4" (10 cm) in Stockinette stitch (St st)

ABBREVIATIONS
C5F: Slip 2 sts to cn, hold to front, k3, k2 from cn.
LT: Knit into back of second st, then knit first and second sts together through back loops, slip both sts from left-hand needle together.
RT: K2tog, but do not drop sts from left-hand needle, insert right-hand needle between 2 sts just worked and knit first st again, slip both sts from left-hand needle together.

KEY

☐ **Knit**

⊡ **Purl**

Ⓡ **K1-tbl**

◺◹ **LT:** Knit into back of second st, then knit first and second sts together through back loops, slip both sts from left-hand needle together.

◸◿ **RT:** K2tog, but do not drop sts from left-hand needle, insert right-hand needle between 2 sts just worked and knit first st again, slip both sts from left-hand needle together.

◁────▷ **C5F:** Slip 2 sts to cn, hold to front, k3, k2 from cn.

PATTERN B

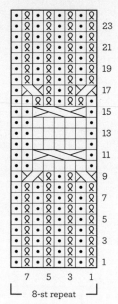

7   5   3   1

⌐──── 8-st repeat ────⌐

STITCH PATTERNS

PATTERN A

(multiple of 8 sts)

Rnds 1-8: *K1-tbl, p1; repeat from * to end.

Rnd 9: *LT, k1-tbl, p1, k1-tbl, RT, p1; repeat from * to end.

Rnds 10 and 12-14: *P1, k5, p2; repeat from * to end.

Rnds 11 and 15: *P1, C5F, p2; repeat from * to end.

Rnd 16: *P1, [k1-tbl] twice, p1, [k1-tbl] twice, p2; repeat from * to end.

Rnd 17: *RT, k1-tbl, p1, k1-tbl, LT, p1; repeat from * to end.

Rnds 18-24: Repeat Rnd 1.

LEG

CO 32 sts. Divide sts evenly among 4 needles (8-8-8-8). Join for working in the rnd, being careful not to twist sts; place marker (pm) for beginning of rnd. Begin Pattern A; work even for 24 rnds.

HEEL FLAP

Set-Up Row 1 (RS): [K1-tbl, p1] 4 times, turn.

Set-Up Row 2: Slip 1, p15, working all 16 sts onto 1 needle for Heel Flap, and removing marker. Leave remaining 16 sts on 2 needles for instep.

Row 1: Working only on 16 Heel Flap sts, *slip 1, k1; repeat from * to end.

Row 2: Slip 1, purl to end.

Repeat Rows 1 and 2 four times.

TURN HEEL

Set-Up Row 1 (RS): Slip 1, k9, skp, turn.

Set-Up Row 2: Slip 1, p4, p2tog, turn.

Row 1: Slip 1, knit to 1 st before gap, skp (the 2 sts on either side of gap), turn.

Row 2: Slip 1, purl to 1 st before gap, p2tog (the 2 sts on either side of gap), turn.

Rows 3 and 4: Repeat Rows 1 and 2.

Rows 5: Slip 1, knit to 1 st before gap, k1, turn.

Row 6: Slip 1, purl to 1 st before gap, p1, turn–8 sts remain.

GUSSET

Next Row (RS): *Needle 1:* Knit across Heel Flap sts, pick up and knit 6 sts along left side of Heel Flap, M1; *Needles 2 and 3:* Knit across sts on instep needles; *Needle 4:* M1, pick up and knit 6 sts along right side of Heel Flap, k3 from Needle 1. Join for working in the rnd; pm for beginning of rnd–38 sts (11-8-8-11).

Next Rnd: *Needle 1:* Knit to last 2 sts, skp; *Needles 2 and 3:* Knit; *Needle 4:* K2tog, knit to end–36 sts remain.

Decrease Rnd: *Needle 1:* Knit to last 3 sts, skp, k1; *Needles 2 and 3:* Knit; *Needle 4:* K1, k2tog, knit to end–34 sts remain. Repeat Decrease Rnd once–32 sts remain (8-8-8-8). Work even for 1 rnd.

FOOT

Work even until Foot measures 8½", or 1½" less than desired length from back of Heel.

TOE

Decrease Rnd: *Needle 1:* Knit to last 3 sts, skp, k1; *Needle 2:* K1, k2tog, knit to end; *Needle 3:* Knit to last 3 sts, skp, k1; *Needle 4:* K1, k2tog, knit to end–28 sts remain. Knit 1 rnd.

Repeat Decrease Rnd every other rnd 4 times–12 sts remain (3-3-3-3). Knit to end of Needle 1.

FINISHING

Break yarn, leaving long tail. Transfer sts from Needle 1 to Needle 4, and sts from Needle 3 to Needle 2. Using Kitchener st (see General Techniques, page 140), graft Toe sts. Weave in ends. Block lightly.

sayonara

Sayonara is the Japanese farewell, or
word for "good-bye." I include these
over-the-knee socks here as a sort of
"long" good-bye as we are at the
end of the pattern section of the book.
Worked in light worsted-weight yarn, the
socks feature a simple cable pattern
with a literal twist: one "strand" of the
cable is itself composed of twisted
stitches, lending a complex look without
much added difficulty. The pattern is fun
to knit and hard to stop—hence the
length of the socks. They are topped off
by a twisted rib in a contrasting color.

FINISHED MEASUREMENTS
7½" Foot circumference
10" Foot length from back of Heel
24½" Leg length to base of Heel,
with Cuff unfolded

YARN
Crystal Palace Yarns Merino 5 (100% superwash
merino wool; 50 grams / 110 yards): 5 balls #5222
Rosewood (MC); 1 ball #5220 Flame (A)

NEEDLES
One 16" (40 cm) circular (circ)
needle size US 5 (3.75 mm)
One set of five double-pointed needles
(dpn) size US 4 (3.5 mm)
Change needle size if necessary to
obtain correct gauge.

NOTIONS
Stitch marker; cable needle (cn)

GAUGE
21 sts and 30 rnds = 4" (10 cm) in Stockinette
stitch (St st), using smaller needles

ABBREVIATIONS
RT: K2tog, but do not drop sts from left-hand
needle, insert right-hand needle between 2 sts
just worked and knit first st again, slip both
sts from left-hand needle together.
C4B: Slip 2 sts to cn, hold to back, k2,
k2 from cn.

STITCH PATTERNS

PATTERN A
(multiple of 2 sts; 1-rnd repeat)
All Rnds: *K1-tbl, p1; repeat from *
to end.

PATTERN B
(multiple of 11 sts; 16-rnd repeat)
Rnds 1 and 9: *P3, C4B, p3, k1-tbl;
repeat from * to end.
**Rnd 2 and All Even-Numbered
Rnds:** *P3, k4, p3, k1-tbl; repeat
from * to end.
Rnds 3, 5, and 7: *P3, RT, k2, p3,
k1-tbl; repeat from * to end.
Rnds 11, 13, and 15: *P3, k2, RT, p3,
k1-tbl; repeat from * to end.
Rnd 16: Repeat Rnd 2.
Repeat Rnds 1-16 for Pattern B.

LEG
*Note: Change to dpn when necessary
for number of sts on needle.*
Using circ needle and A, CO 74 sts.
Join for working in the rnd, being
careful not to twist sts; place
marker (pm) for beginning of rnd.
Begin Pattern A; work even for
17 rnds.
Next Rnd: Change to MC. K4,
work Pattern B over 66 sts, k4.
Work even for 7 rnds.
Shape Calf: Continuing in pattern
as established, decrease 2 sts this
rnd, then every 8 rnds 10 times, as
follows: Work 2 sts together, work
to last 2 sts, work 2 sts together–44
sts remain.
*Note: To maintain rib pattern while
decreasing, if second st of rnd is a
knit st, work k2tog; if second st is a
purl st, work p2tog. If next-to-last st
of rnd is a knit st, work skp; if
next-to-last st is a purl st, work
p2tog. If you are unable to work a
complete cable cross on Rnds 1 or
9, work remaining cable sts in St st.*

Work even until piece measures
21½" from the beginning. Knit 1
rnd, decrease 1 st on each needle–
40 sts remain (10-10-10-10).

HEEL FLAP
Set-Up Row 1 (RS): K10, turn.
Set-Up Row 2: Slip 1, p19, working
all 20 sts onto 1 needle for Heel
Flap, and removing marker. Leave
remaining 20 sts on 2 needles
for instep.
Row 1: Working only on 20 Heel
Flap sts, *slip 1, k1; repeat from *
to end.
Row 2: Slip 1, purl to end.
Repeat Rows 1 and 2 nine times.

TURN HEEL
Set-Up Row 1 (RS): Slip 1, k11, skp,
k1, turn.
Set-Up Row 2: Slip 1, p5, p2tog,
p1, turn.
Row 1: Slip 1, knit to 1 st before
gap, skp (the 2 sts on either side of
gap), k1, turn.
Row 2: Slip 1, purl to 1 st before
gap, p2tog (the 2 sts on either side
of gap), p1, turn.
Repeat Rows 1 and 2 twice, omitting
final k1 and p1 sts in last repeat of
Rows 1 and 2–12 sts remain.

GUSSET

Next Row (RS): *Needle 1:* Knit across Heel Flap sts, pick up and knit 11 sts along left side of Heel Flap, M1; *Needles 2 and 3:* Knit across sts on instep needles; *Needle 4:* M1, pick up and knit 11 sts along right side of heel flap, k6 from Needle 1. Join for working in the rnd; pm for beginning of rnd—56 sts (18-10-10-18).

Next Rnd: *Needle 1:* Knit to last 2 sts, skp; *Needles 2 and 3:* Knit; *Needle 4:* K2tog, knit to end—54 sts remain.

Decrease Rnd: *Needle 1:* Knit to last 3 sts, skp, k1; *Needles 2 and 3:* Knit; *Needle 4:* K1, k2tog, knit to end—52 sts remain (16-10-10-16). Work even for 1 rnd.

Repeat Decrease Rnd every other rnd 6 times—40 sts remain (10-10-10-10).

FOOT

Work even until Foot measures 8½", or 1½" less than desired length from back of Heel.

TOE

Decrease Rnd: *Needle 1:* Knit to last 3 sts, skp, k1; *Needle 2:* K1, k2tog, knit to end; *Needle 3:* Knit to last 3 sts, skp, k1; *Needle 4:* K1, k2tog, knit to end—36 sts remain. Knit 1 rnd.

Repeat Decrease Rnd every other rnd 5 times—16 sts remain (4-4-4-4). Knit to end of Needle 1.

FINISHING

Break yarn, leaving long tail. Transfer sts from Needle 1 to Needle 4, and sts from Needle 3 to Needle 2. Using Kitchener st (see General Techniques, page 140), graft Toe sts. Weave in ends. Block lightly.

KEY

☐ **Knit**

⊡ **Purl**

⊠ **K1-tbl**

▨ **RT:** K2tog, but do not drop sts from left-hand needle, insert right-hand needle between 2 sts just worked and knit first st again, slip both sts from left-hand needle together.

▧ **C4B:** Slip 2 sts to cn, hold to back, k2, k2 from cn.

PATTERN B

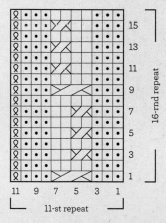

11-st repeat — 16-rnd repeat

general techniques, abbreviations, and sources

CABLE CO

Make a loop (using a slipknot) with the working yarn and place it on the left-hand needle (first st CO), knit into slipknot, draw up a loop but do not drop st from left-hand needle; place new loop on left-hand needle; *insert the tip of the right-hand needle into the space between the last 2 sts on the left-hand needle and draw up a loop; place the loop on the left-hand needle. Repeat from * for remaining sts to be CO, or for casting on at the end of a row in progress.

KITCHENER STITCH

Using a blunt yarn needle, thread a length of yarn approximately 4 times the length of the section to be joined. Hold the pieces to be joined wrong sides together, with the needles holding the sts parallel, both ends pointing to the right. Working from right to left, insert yarn needle into first st on front needle as if to purl, pull yarn through, leaving st on needle; insert yarn needle into first st on back needle as if to knit, pull yarn through, leaving st on needle; *insert yarn needle into first st on front needle as if to knit, pull yarn through, remove st from needle; insert yarn needle into next st on front needle as if to purl, pull yarn through, leave st on needle; insert yarn needle into first st on back needle as if to purl, pull yarn through, remove st from needle; insert yarn needle into next st on back needle as if to knit, pull yarn through, leave st on needle. Repeat from *, working 3 or 4 sts at a time, then go back and adjust tension to match the pieces being joined. When 1 st remains on each needle, cut yarn and pass through last 2 sts to fasten off.

Long-Tail (Thumb) CO

Leaving tail with about 1" of yarn for each st to be cast on, make a slipknot in the yarn and place it on the right-hand needle, with the end to the front and the working end to the back. Insert the thumb and forefinger of your left hand between the strands of yarn so that the working end is around your forefinger, and the tail end is around your thumb "slingshot" fashion; *insert the tip of the right-hand needle into the front loop on the thumb, hook the strand of yarn coming from the forefinger from back to front, and draw it through the loop on your thumb; remove your thumb from the loop and pull on the working yarn to tighten the new st on the right-hand needle; return your thumb and forefinger to their original positions, and repeat from * for remaining sts to be CO.

Reading Charts

Unless otherwise specified in the instructions, when working straight, charts are read from right to left for RS rows, from left to right for WS rows. Row numbers are written at the beginning of each row. Numbers on the right indicate RS rows; numbers on the left indicate WS rows. When working circular, all rounds are read from right to left.

Short Row Shaping

Work the number of sts specified in the instructions, wrap and turn (wrp-t) as follows:

To wrap a knit stitch, bring yarn to the front (purl position), slip the next st purlwise to the right-hand needle, bring yarn to the back of work, return the slipped st on the right-hand needle to the left-hand

needle; turn, ready to work the next row, leaving the remaining sts unworked. To wrap a purl stitch, work as for wrapping a knit stitch, but bring the yarn to the back (knit position) before slipping the stitch, and to the front after slipping the stitch.

When short rows are completed, or when working progressively longer short rows, work the wrap together with the wrapped st as you come to it as follows:

If st is to be worked as a knit st, insert the right-hand needle into the wrap, from below, then into the wrapped st; k2tog; if st to be worked is a purl st, insert needle into the wrapped st, then down into the wrap; p2tog. (Wrap may be lifted onto the left-hand needle, then worked together with the wrapped st if this is easier.)

Three-Needle BO

Place the sts to be joined onto 2 same-size needles; hold the pieces to be joined with the right sides facing each other and the needles parallel. Holding both needles in your left hand, using working yarn and a third needle same size or one size larger, insert third needle into first st on front needle, then into first st on back needle; knit these 2 sts together; *knit next st from each needle together (2 sts on right-hand needle); pass first st over second st to BO 1 st. Repeat from * until 1 st remains on third needle; cut yarn and fasten off.

abbreviations

BO Bind off

Circ Circular

Cn Cable needle

CO Cast on

Dpn Double-pointed needle(s)

K Knit

K2tog Knit 2 sts together.

K3tog Knit 3 sts together.

K4tog Knit 4 sts together.

K1-tbl Knit 1 stitch through the back loop.

MB Make bobble (as instructed).

M1 or M1-l (make 1-left slanting) With the tip of the left-hand needle inserted from front to back, lift the strand between the 2 needles onto the left-hand needle; knit the strand through the back loop to increase 1 st.

M1-r (make 1-right slanting) With the tip of the left-hand needle inserted from back to front, lift the strand between the 2 needles onto the left-hand needle; knit it through the front loop to increase 1 st.

P Purl

P2tog Purl 2 sts together.

Pm Place marker.

Psso (pass slipped stitch over) Pass slipped st on right-hand needle over the sts indicated in the instructions, as in binding off.

Rnd Round

RS Right side

S2kp2 Slip next 2 sts together to right-hand needle as if to knit 2 together, k1, pass 2 slipped sts over.

S3kp3 Slip next 3 sts together to right-hand needle as if to knit 3 together, k1, pass 3 slipped sts over.

Skp (slip, knit, pass) Slip next st knitwise to right-hand needle, k1, pass slipped st over knit st.

Sk2p (double decrease) Slip next st knitwise to right-hand needle, k2tog, pass slipped st over st from k2tog.

Ssk (slip, slip, knit) Slip next 2 sts to right-hand needle one at a time as if to knit; return them to left-hand needle one at a time in their new orientation; knit them together through the back loop(s).

Ssp (slip, slip, purl) Slip next 2 sts to right-hand needle one at a time as if to knit; return them to left-hand needle one at a time in their new orientation; purl them together through the back loops.

St(s) Stitch(es)

Tbl Through the back loop

Tog Together

WS Wrong side

Wrp-t Wrap and turn (see Short Row Shaping, page 141).

Wyib With yarn in back

Yo Yarnover

sources

YARN

ALPACA WITH A TWIST
866-37-TWIST
www.alpacawithatwist.com

BLUE SKY ALPACAS
888-460-8862
www.blueskyalpacas.com

BROWN SHEEP COMPANY
800-826-9136
www.brownsheep.com

CHERRY TREE HILL YARN
802-525-3311
www.cherryyarn.com

CRYSTAL PALACE YARNS
510-237-9988
www.straw.com

ELANN.COM INC
604-952-4096
www.elann.com

FAIRMOUNT FIBERS
(Distributors of
Manos del Uruguay)
888-566-9970
www.fairmountfibers.com

IMPERIAL STOCK RANCH
542-395-2507
www.imperialstockranch.com

JOJOLAND INTERNATIONAL, LLC
972-624-8990
www.jojoland.com

KNIT ONE, CROCHET TOO
207-892-9625
www.knitonecrochettoo.com

KNIT PICKS
800-574-1323
www.knitpicks.com

**KNITTING FEVER
INTERNATIONAL, LLC**
516-546-3600
www.knittingfever.com

KOLLAGE YARNS
888-829-7758
www.kollageyarns.com

LION BRAND YARN
800-258-YARN
www.lionbrand.com

**LISA SOUZA KNITWEAR AND
DYEWORKS**
530-647-1183
www.lisaknit.com

LORNA'S LACES
773-935-3803
www.lornaslaces.net

SCHAEFER YARN COMPANY
800-367-9276
www.schaeferyarn.com

SHIBUIKNITS, LLC
503-595-5898
www.shibuiknits.com

S.R. KERTZER
800-263-2354
www.kertzer.com

WESTMINSTER FIBERS, INC.
800-445-9276
www.westminsterfibers.com

JAPANESE STITCH PATTERN BOOKS

LACIS
510-843-7178
www.lacis.com

THE NEEDLE ARTS BOOK SHOP
888-860-3338
www.needleartsbookshop.com

acknowledgments

I first want to thank my editor, Melanie Falick, for helping me to create a collection of socks to appeal to a wide range of knitters by reminding me (repeatedly) to diversify the colors and weights of yarns, as well as the sock styles, and to stick mostly to solid-colored yarns so that the stitch patterns would really show up.

My friend and pattern tester, Barbara Kinney, tested each and every pattern as I wrote it. Sue McCain tech-edited my patterns and created the charts. Betty Christiansen edited the nonpattern text. I want to thank all of them for their patience with a new author. Hopefully, in spite of us being mere mortals, there aren't any errors in this book.

My gratitude also goes out to photographer Yoko Inoue, photo-stylist Yuki Matsuo, and graphic designer Sarah Von Dreele for presenting my work in such a lovely fashion.

I must also thank Virginia McLaurin, the owner of my local yarn shop, Loopville Yarns, in Knoxville, Tennessee. It was "Jinka" who kept telling me that I should write a book, and I finally took her advice when I realized that the Japanese stitch patterns would make it different from all the other sock books on the shelves.